How To Set Up & Maintain a BETTER Voiceover Business

Gabrielle Nistico

This book is the licensed property of Three Moon Media LLC. Any improper, unauthorized re- printing of this material is strictly prohibited.

Copyright © 2017 Three Moon Media

Author, Gabrielle Nistico
Editor, Eric Schwabenlender
Assistant Editors, Lewis Banks and Shelly Murphy
Cover Design, Brandon Falls

First printed 2010 Printed in the United States of America
Published by Three Moon Media
Third edition

900 Mt. Holly Holly-Huntersville Rd.
Charlotte, NC 28214

www.GabrielleNistico.com
704-674-8294

Acknowledgements

The author would like to acknowledge the following individuals for their hard work, dedication and support of this book: Adam Goodman, Eric Simendinger, Brandon Falls, Chris Thomas, Lewis Banks (LewisBanksVO.com), Shelly Murphy, Alisha Fleming and Angelique Coppernoll.

This book is dedicated to all of the creative, artistic, right-brain thinkers who have come to me for business guidance over the years. It is my sincere hope that with this book, I'll aid you in wrangling and harnessing your creative power so that you can kick butt and take names! It's my goal to help you move in a more balanced direction, so that your entrepreneurial skills will more effectively match your voiceover talent.

About this Book

This book is intended for new and existing VO talent. It will help you to sharpen your business skills so that you can become a better entrepreneur who is capable of running a more successful voiceover business.

The material in this book is a collection of common and critical managerial essentials. It has been compiled especially for voiceover artists who are great performers, yet find it difficult to efficiently handle tasks such as billing, collections, marketing, sales and promotions.

If you are one of the many who has struggled with these challenges, this book will prove to be an excellent investment in your voiceover career.

Gabrielle Nistico is a voiceover actress, coach, marketing consultant, demo creator and web designer with 100% focus on all things voiceover. Gabby is available for free 30 minute consultations. She welcomes your feedback and questions.

Dear Reader,

When I first started offering business and marketing training in the voiceover industry there was a massive hole in the marketplace. Some days it seemed like everyone and their brother was teaching voiceover performance and offering voiceover lessons. But no one – absolutely no one – was teaching the business of voiceover until I started offering those classes in 2008. I was the first voiceover business coach.

The need for these services was palpable and voiceover actors were begging for business training and guidance. Along with my passion for marketing, branding, and the business side of the industry - this sparked a whole new era of training.

Now there are a plethora of voiceover coaches offering similar services with varying levels of results. What I find is that thorough details are a must in voiceover business training or you'll find yourself with a limited amount of information that will keep you coming back time and time again for more classes. This is a good business model for a coach, but not for you and your wallet.

My continued commitment to telling "the whole story" regarding how to brand, market, and sell your services is why voiceover actors like yourself choose to work with me. Oh yeah – that, and my methods work.

Thank you for choosing this book and to work with "The Business FIRST Voiceover Coach," the first of all the business voiceover coaches. Let's get started…

This workbook is designed to help you understand and organize the essential administrative needs of your VO business so that you can confidently set up and run your company like a pro. I know that running any business is not easy. However, I believe that voice talents have it especially rough. The average talent is a one-man or one-woman outfit. Servicing clients, finding leads, prospecting for jobs, auditioning and scheduling sessions is a full- time job already.

Since most VO talent tend to be right brain thinkers (creative people), these important processes can become overwhelming, which inevitably leads to procrastination and/or neglect. Talent have to work extra hard to make sure that the administration of their business does not fall by the wayside. Even marketing (a task that on the surface seems very creative) is really all about effective strategy, planning, and analyzing. These types of administrative duties should be seen not as chores but rather the very foundation and infrastructure of your business.

Managing these tasks does not have to be daunting. Some simple planning will ensure that as your business grows, you don't fall behind. Being prepared now will safe-guard your personal life from being adversely affected by working long hours, weekends, evenings, or by having to play catch-up in the future.

I can't stress enough how critical it is that you stay organized. Creating a task-oriented schedule and maintaining an organized office from today forward will keep you cool, confident, and most importantly - working. By following this workbook and using my guidelines to the fullest, you will find yourself far better off than your chaotic VO brethren.

Oh, and one more thing - in order to make it in business, YOU MUST STOP ACTING LIKE AN ACTOR. I wish you great success and a profitable endeavor.

Gabby Nistico

BONUS AUDIO

www.soundcloud.com/
thevoiceovervixen/businessbook

Table of Contents

Chapter 1 - Getting Started 9
   Essential Items for Your VO Business 10
   Operations: Time Management 12

Chapter 2 Accounting 16
   Accounting – Part I: To Incorporate or Not 17
   Accounting – Part II: Business Checking Account . . 21
   Accounting – Part III: Accounting Policies 23
   Accounting – Part V: More on Accounts Receivable. . 30
   Collections 35
   Tax Deductions 40

Chapter 3 - Daily Operations 42
   Contact Management 43
   Outsourcing 46
   Contracts 49
   Budgeting For Success. 52

Chapter 4 - Branding & Marketing 54
   Increasing Profits with Marketing and Sales 55
   Promotions, Branding and Marketing 60
   Marketing Misconceptions 62
   Branding When I'm Brand New 77
   More on Websites 80
   Social Networking. 84
   Social Networking Part 2 86

Chapter 5 - Sales. 88
   Cold Calling and Sales – It's Time to Smile and Dial. . 89
   Pay To Play Basics 94

Chapter 6 - Staying Focused. 102
   Business: A Judgment Free Work Zone 103
   Desperation Stay Away 106
   The Economy of Voiceovers 109
   The True Cost of Success. 111
   Setting S.M.A.R.T Goals 114
   Recommended Products 117
   Helpful Apps. 120

Chapter 7 - Voiceover Agents 122
   Intro to Agents 123
   Union Agents, Non Union, or Both 131
   Legalities Know How to Pick a Legit Agent 134
   Presentation: Perception Matters Most 136
   A Word from Your Peers 142
   The Art of Voice Acting – on Agents 144
   Sept. 2013 - Backstage.com. 145
   The Rules to Follow 152
   How to Find Agents 155

This workbook is focused solely on running a VO business. It is assumed that you already have items pertaining to performance, such as demos and training. If you do not or you need assistance acquiring those products, please contact the author for help.
You may also benefit from her book, VO 101 – Everything You Need To Know To Start A Voiceover Career.
It is available for purchase at www.GabrielleNistico.com

Chapter 1
Getting Started

Essential Items for Your VO Business

Individual needs may vary – not all items will be critical to obtain right away or at all. Keep track of what you have and what you need for the future with this checklist.

General Business Operations			
O	A relatively new computer with memory, storage and operating system to support your business needs		
O	Business licenses and articles of incorporation		
O	Business software for word processing, databases, spreadsheets, and contact management. (Microsoft Office Suite recommended)		
O	High-speed internet	O	EIN number from IRS
O	Telephone line with voicemail / business cell phone		
Accounting			
O	Invoices with your company logo, payment and contact info		
O	General accounting ledger and/or accounting software		
O	Business Checking Account	O	Collection Letters
Tax Accounting			
O	Tax software, online tax service or an accountant		
O	Electronic or paper method for storing expense receipts		
O	Address of state office that receives your annual report – found at Secretary of State website for the state of your incorporation		
Marketing			
O	Website and E-mail account	O	Photo, Bio and Logo
O	Business Cards	O	P.O. Box
Computer Maintenance			
O	Anti-virus software to remove spyware, viruses and to regularly clean your system		

O	External hard drive or cloud service to back up your computer
O	Telephone numbers for technical support centers and local IT computer repair company
O	A firebox for safe storage of backup and important documents
Contact Management	
O	File cabinet, spreadsheet, or software for client records / paid jobs
O	Performance spreadsheet or software to track auditions and callbacks
O	General contact management software
Additional Items	

Use the "Additional Items" section to track other items your business needs – including studio equipment, marketing material and VO training and coaching

Operations: Time Management / Working from Home

Time management is a challenge for all business-people, not just VO talent. But I sympathize with VO talent because I know working from home is not easy. There are so many distractions!

The first big step towards running a better VO business is to assess how you use your time. You must establish a standard set of business hours and remain dedicated to those dates and times with few if any, exceptions. Post clear hours of operation for yourself and your clients.

During those work hours, you must make a diligent effort to clear away distractions. This is where working from home has its biggest disadvantage. The laundry can wait. You don't need to check the mail box until evening. You can call your friend back in the evening too. Everything unrelated to business must wait. How you use your hours has the biggest impact on the success of your business.

If you were commuting to an office every day, this is exactly how your life would operate. Personal chores, duties, responsibilities, etc., would take place AFTER work. Working from home does not give you carte blanche to take care of personal matters whenever you want. You must reserve work hours for work tasks. You may also need to make this clear to other members of your household. It's easy for spouses and significant others to take your at-home / at-work time for granted. They may think that working from home means greater flexibility. In actuality, it rarely does.

Now it's time to organize and plan the use of your operational hours so that you maintain a consistent and focused schedule. What's the first thing you should schedule? LUNCH. No, really. It's very easy for self-employed individuals to forget to take breaks. Give yourself some personal time while on the job. Schedule a consistent lunch hour, as well as two 15 minute breaks; one in the morning and one in the afternoon.

Next, dissect the remainder of your day into specific actions and duties. You must designate daily blocks of time for:

Prospecting new leads / clients.
Marketing.
Auditioning.
Accounting and collections.
Phone calls.
And_____.

Some tasks will be of daily importance, others will be of weekly, bi-weekly or monthly importance. So create daily, weekly and monthly rules for your time.

Whatever you do, don't over-schedule your day. Leave yourself the flexibility to change and rearrange items because paid work will always take priority over any scheduled task. So, if you over-manage your time, you will constantly feel behind and stressed.

Next is a sample schedule, followed by a blank schedule so that you may fill in your own tasks. Do not fill it out until you have read this entire workbook and know all the day-to-day tasks you must accomplish.

SAMPLE SCHEDULE
Monday – Friday

9am: Check emails, file papers, organize the day.

10am: Cold calling, prospecting, and other sales duties.

11:45am – Take a 15 minute break

12pm: Answer Auditions

1 pm: Lunch

2 pm: Marketing and promotions

3:45 pm: Take a 15 minute break

4 pm: Accounting

5 pm: Answer Auditions

Weekly

Tuesday - Collections

Thursday - Contact management

Friday – Social network maintenance

Monthly

1st of the month – Promotions / Press Releases

15th of the month – Update Website

Time Management Worksheet

Monday - Friday

Time	Action:

Weekly Tasks

Weekday	Task:

Monthly Tasks

Recurring Date	Task:

Chapter 2
Accounting

Accounting – Part I: To Incorporate or Not

If you don't have a corporate license and you are currently working in VO, or if you have recently launched a VO company, (without a corporate license) you are classified by the federal government as a sole-proprietor. This means you are the sole owner of a company that operates under your social security number. You and you alone are responsible for this entity, legally and financially.

Let me make this perfectly clear. There is nothing "wrong" with being a sole-proprietor. In fact, if you are currently employed by another company and VO is a part-time effort for you, sole-proprietorship is likely an ideal situation.

The expenses of owning and operating your VO business can greatly offset the taxes you pay on your W-2 earnings. Of course, the flip-side to this is that if your voice business is doing very well and you have another source of income, you may owe money on your taxes.

As a sole-proprietor, your company is legitimate as long as your accounting is in good order. Most banks will allow you to open a business checking account as a sole-proprietor under a business name of your choosing. It is essential that you do so in order to keep your business spending and earnings separate from your personal finances.

In some counties, you may need to apply for an Assumed Name Certificate, which allows you to accept checks in your business's name. Your local bank will be able to inform you of your county's requirements.

Many voiceover actors operate their business as a sole-proprietorship simply because there is little to no liability in being a VO business owner. You likely have no employees and you likely work from home in a private studio that has no foot traffic, walk-ins or on-location appointments.

Chances are your "assistant" is your spouse or your pet. You don't have any inventory or merchandise either; and there is therefore little chance of someone creating a legal dispute over your services. In fact, it would most likely be you making a legal claim against a client; with the most likely scenario being that someone fails to pay one of your invoices.

VO talent do have a few choices when it comes to incorporating their business. You may create an "LLC" (Limited Liability Corporation) or a "C- Class" corporation. I recommend that you become an LLC simply because, again, you have very little liability in what you do.

The primary benefit to owning a corporation is that your personal finances and assets are completely separated from your business's finances and assets. The corporation stands alone legally and financially. I recommend that you incorporate your VO business if: it is your only source of income or if you earn more than $20,000 a year in VO.

The process of incorporating is very simple. DO NOT be suckered into paying big bucks to incorporation companies that advertise their services online and on TV. They charge far too much money for something you can do on your own.

You do not need any assistance in setting up a corporation. Simply use the internet to look up the secretary of state's office for the state you live in and request the forms needed to create your corporation.

There is usually a fee to incorporate or to create an LLC (ranging from $100-$400) and each year you will also pay an annual report fee that keeps your business license active and prevents the corporation from dissolving. This is literally the "cost of doing business" in your state.

On the next page you will find a chart of some recent fees in all 50 states to give you an idea. Please remember that these fees are always subject to change, so be sure to check your states local website.

Fees for Incorporation / LLC Formation**

State	INC	LLC	State	INC	LLC
AL	165	165	MO	58	50
AK	250	250	MT	70	70
AZ	60	50	NE	65	120
AR	50	50	NV	75	75
CA	105	75	NH	100	100
CO	50	50	NJ	125	125
CT	455	175	NM	100	50
DE	140	140	NY	145	210
DC	220	220	NC	125	125
FL	155	78.75	ND	100	135
GA	100	100	OH	125	125
HI	50	50	OK	52	104
ID	101	100	OR	100	100
IL	175	500	PA	125	125
IN	90	90	RI	230	150
IA	50	50	SC	135	110
KS	90	160	SD	150	150
KY	55	55	TN	125	325
LA	100	100	TX	310	310
ME	145	175	UT	72	72
MD	155	155	VT	125	125
MA	295	520	VA	79	104
MI	60	50	WA	200	200
MN	160	160	WV	82	132
MS	50	50	WI	100	130
			WY	103	103

*** Fees are always subject to change.*
You'll want to look up your state's current fees online.

Accounting – Part II: Business Checking Account

Whether you incorporate or not, you will need to open a business checking account in order to properly maintain your accounting. I outlined the process of opening a business checking account as a sole-proprietor in the previous section.

If you incorporate, you'll need to obtain an Employer Identification Number (EIN) from the IRS, to open a business checking account. You can obtain one at www.IRS.gov. An EIN acts like a social security number for your company. Your bank will use this number to issue bank accounts that the company owns and is responsible for.

Your business checking account should be used for business purposes only. You can use it to deposit company earnings and pay business bills. Be sure to research available low or no-cost business checking accounts in your area. You want a bank that does not require a minimum balance and one that won't charge you fees for regular transactions.

Your bank will also provide a business ATM or check card that will allow you to track your business expenses via online banking. Make certain to store electronic or paper copies of your monthly business checking account statements. They will be very helpful when you itemize your expenses at tax time.

Your bank may have an option that will allow you to set up monthly statements that automatically itemize your business expenses by categories you choose. If your bank offers this service, take advantage of it!

Linking your business accounts to your personal accounts is

easy, provided that you use the same bank for both account types. This will allow you to easily transfer money to yourself. By linking these two accounts, you won't have to write yourself a check each pay-day. What's more, it significantly cuts down on the time it takes for you to be able to access the money / salary you pay yourself.

Your salary may fluctuate and that is okay. You are not required to pay yourself a set amount of money. The money you do pay yourself will be recorded on your taxes as Officer or Owner Compensation.

When you fill out your business taxes, you will file a "Schedule K", which allows you to report earnings that you paid yourself. That, in turn, becomes the money you report on your personal taxes. Make sure that you keep detailed records of all the amounts you pay yourself so that you can accurately tabulate your earnings. Keep those separate from your company expenses.

Notes: *Use the space below to write notes or reminders related to business banking.*

_____
_____
_____
_____
_____
_____
_____
_____
_____

Accounting – Part III: Accounting Policies

Once your business checking account is set up you can begin to plan your business's policies and procedures with regard to accounting.

Even if you are just starting your voice career, planning ahead will prevent disorganization and poor time management later. Disorder with foundational items like accounting can result in major business pit falls in the future. In this section, I will help you set up a proper accounting infrastructure that can grow and evolve along with your business.

Accounting can seem cumbersome, especially if you have an allergic reaction every time you see too many numbers. Hiring a CPA is great if you can afford one and if you know a professional you trust. With or without a CPA, here are the simplest ways to achieve accounting balance.

Rely on the basic economic skills you probably learned in high school to handle your company's accounting and taxable records. Every penny must be accounted for. Basic business accounting consists of 2 main parts, Accounts Receivable (money in) and Accounts Payable (money out). Items that fall under accounts payable are bills you must pay from anyone who supplied you with a product or service.

Most companies refer to payable parties as "vendors". Vendors that are directly related to your business's operating expenses can include utility companies, internet and phone, and other service providers, etc. It is important that you keep excellent records of all business bills and any party to whom you owe money.

Accounts receivable is the money owed to you for work you performed. It's the best kind of accounting there is! Use your business checking account to track accounts payable and receivable activity. Keep meticulous hand-written records in a business check registry or electronically in a spreadsheet. This process is referred to as your General Ledger.

Every month, you must balance your company books to zero. Every penny must be accounted for and profits must be carried over to the new term. If you do this monthly, your taxes will be easier to calculate and you won't be attempting to reconcile transactions from the distant past. Don't postpone your accounting duties! Procrastination will lead to black holes in your books and tax records.

The money calculated in your accounts receivables (money you earn) that is greater than your accounts payable (money you spend) is called Gross Profit. Gross profit serves as an excellent indicator of how well your business is doing.

You may experience a negative gross profit at first. This means that more money is being spent than is being earned. It's not uncommon for business owners to use their personal finances or a line of credit to fulfill their accounts payable when a company is still in its infancy.

If you plan on using a credit card to make purchases and help fund your company, you must keep credit card statements too, as they will aid in the justification of your expenses at tax time. The next few pages show you an example of an Excel spreadsheet used for book-keeping.

Microsoft Excel is a powerful numeric database software that can greatly assist in the task of managing your business accounting and building a general ledger. Excel has "tabs" that allow you to keep multiple, corresponding spreadsheets saved in the same document. Excel lets you sort information quickly in organized columns. What's more, it lets you add sums super-fast and it's expandable. As your business grows, your Excel spreadsheets will grow with you. The benefits of Excel are really impressive once you become comfortable with the program. Consider taking a community college course in Excel or purchase the book Excel for Dummies.

INVOICE TRACKER

Date:	Deposited:	Withdrawn:	Balance:	Invoice #:	Check #:	Vendor:	Tax Category:
4/26/16	$500		$500	TL0398	7895		Business Income
4/27/16		$300	$200		984	AudioTech	Equipment
5/1/16	$300		$500	SF35752	3546		Business Income
5/3/16		$500	$0		1465	AT&T	Telecomunication
5/4/16	$800		$800	SM6598	4466		Business Income
5/4/16	$200		$1000	RG498756	8124		Business Income
5/6/16		$800	$200		5421	Best Buy	Equipment
5/7/16	$150		$350	RCM9981	620		Business Income
5/8/16		$200	$150		0254	TJ Landscaping	Maintenance
5/9/16	$500		$650	MM73610	74298		Business Income

26

GENERAL LEDGER

Job Date:	Invoice #:	Client Name:	Address:	Client Email:	Job:	Amount:	Invoiced:
4/26/16	7895	Shelly Enterprises	123 Sky St. Charlotte, NC	shelly@gmail.com	Narration: 5 pages	$500	4/27/16
4/27/16	984	Chris Productions	123 ABC St. Charleston, SC	chris@gmail.com	Commercial: ABC Client :15	$200	4/28/16
5/1/16	3546	Lewis LLC	123 Euclid Ave. New York, NY	lewis@gmail.com	Audiobook 40 finished hours	$1000	5/2/16
5/3/16	1465	James Corp	123 Main St. Barstow, CA	james@gmail.com	Commercial: ABC Client :30	$500	5/4/16
5/4/16	4466	Raven Recordings	123 Bourbon St. New Orleans, LA	raven@gmail.com	E-learning, 10 pgs	$800	5/5/16
5/4/16	8124	Shelly Enterprises	123 Sky St. Charlotte, NC	shelly@gmail.com	Narration Recuts Script change	$500	5/5/16
5/6/16	5421	Brandon Media	123 South Park Denver, CO	brandon@gmail.com	Commercial: ABC Client :60	$200	5/7/16
5/7/16	620	Dexter Digital	Colony 23 Moon, Milky Way	dexter@gmail.com	ADR Promo ABC, 4 wks	$400	5/8/16
5/8/16	0254	Arya Audio	1 Spark Way Winterfell, Realm	arya@ghost.com	Commercial: ABC Client :30	$150	5/9/16
5/9/16	74298	Dorian Gray LLC	79 Rainy Street Hundred Acre Wood	dorian@gmail.com	Video Game - 3.5hrs Multi- Character	$650	5/10/16

Accounting – Part IV: More on Accounts Payable

A business must know its exact expenses each month. Your next database (or Excel spreadsheet tab) will consist of all your fixed monthly bills. A fixed bill is a bill with an owed amount that doesn't change from month-to- month. An example of a fixed monthly bill would be a business loan payment.

Your third database (or Excel tab) should be a month to month record of discretionary spending. These are items with owed amounts that vary from month to month. Phone bills, credit card payments and utility services all fall into this category.

Non-recurring or periodic overhead and operating expenses such as an equipment purchase, office supplies, advertising expenses, etc., can also be logged on your discretionary spending sheet. As opposed to committed expenses, there is usually room to reduce the amount you put towards discretionary bills.

> Invest in Neat Receipts. If you find it difficult to manage your spending and keep track of piles of receipts, this is your answer. Neat Receipts and similar products are receipt scanners that come with their own intuitive software. It sorts, computes, and categorizes receipts for you in easy-to-use databases.
>
> Neat Receipts saves you the headache of sifting through and sorting hundreds of tax receipts. The best part though, is that you can scan and toss! Neat Receipts is IRS compliant and their scan and sort system is accepted by the IRS. You never have to save a single receipt, just set aside a little time every month to scan them.

Monitoring discretionary spending allows you to see exactly where your money is being spent and how it is allocated according to tax categories. It also gives you an easy way to see the amount being spent on items in a similar category month to month and year to year.

You may also track all of your discretionary spending by reserving the use of a dedicated business credit card for only these purchases. Your monthly statements can serve as a backup of receipts and many credit card companies allow you to itemize your statements online according to accounting and tax categories. For most businesses, all or most of their accounts payable items (both fixed and discretionary) are tax deductible.

A Profit/Loss Statement is the best way to see how your business is doing month to month. Profit is money you've earned minus money you have spent in a given time period. A Loss is when you have spent more money than you have earned. It is normal for most talent's businesses to operate at a loss for the first few months or even years.

Money spent on training, equipment and marketing materials may not pay off until later on. It's important to not give up and try to minimize your expenditures on a monthly basis in order to achieve a profit. With some common sense and an eye for bargains, you can be cash flow positive in less time than you think.

Accounting – Part V: More on Accounts Receivable

The day-to-day activity of Accounts Receivable is very different than that of Accounts Payable. You will need another Excel tab or spreadsheet for receivables as well as several essential forms.

An invoice is the first and most important form. Your clients will need to receive a detailed, well-organized invoice in order to pay you. Your invoice must meet the current standards of your client's accounts payable department.

Clients can/may refuse to pay or delay paying you until they have received a proper invoice. Many business owners feel that an invoice is also an extension of their marketing and branding, so a well presented invoice with your company logo can help promote and legitimize your brand.

Upon completing a job, it is imperative that you send an invoice immediately after you finish the work. This will prevent you from either forgetting a job (yes I know talent who have actually FORGOTTEN to bill a client) or from losing or misplacing important paperwork.

> You can find many customizable invoice templates at Microsoft.com. **Quick-Books** accounting software will supply a variety of invoice template options that you can customize to your need as will **Fresh Books** and **Paypal.**
>
> Whatever you choose, you need to be able to quickly and easily see who owes you money and who has paid in full. Color coding a spreadsheet will make this possible, or you can use software that offers these tracking functions. I use Fresh Books. It's one of the most essentials parts of my day-to-day operation.

Both can result in unnecessary delays in getting paid. Always be sure to ask a client about special invoice requirements such as purchase order numbers. Confirm that your invoice is being sent to the correct person too. Do not assume that it will go to the person who hired you. There may be an accounts payable person or a 3rd party responsible for paying your invoice. You can send invoices via email or regular mail, but most clients prefer email.

Once an invoice is sent, you can usually expect to be paid within 30 days. However, each company is different and because voiceover jobs often include a number of second or third party vendors, it may take 45, 60 or even 90 days before you are paid. Keeping track of who owes you what is essential to making sure you collect all the money you are owed.

Discuss acceptable payment terms with your clients before you perform any work. There are some instances when it will behoove you to ask for payment up-front, in advance of a job.

We recommend that you ask new clients with whom you don't have a relationship to pay up-front for their first job. Most clients will agree to this term. Alternatively, you may ask to hold a credit card number until they can get you a check or other form of payment. In this case, you'll need to send an invoice before you record.

> PayPal is a great way for clients to transfer money to you. You can then withdraw the money to your business checking account. It is free to open a PayPal account, but they do charge small fees, based on a percentage of transactions. You can find more information on the PayPal website at www.Paypal.com.

Always require payment up-front if your client is overseas. In the event of a dispute or if the client refuses to pay, it is virtually impossible to collect from anyone outside the USA. Getting paid up-front eliminates potential problems later.

Billing software like Quick-Books and Fresh Books will also instantly generate invoices for a returning client who is already in your directory of payers. If you are choosing to do your billing without the assistance of billing software, then create separate computer files for each client. Store their corresponding invoices by date order and you'll be able to pull the last invoice and generate a new invoice and invoice number very quickly.

It is also important to have a clear description of the work performed, script title, final length and any other details from the recording. Don't assume that you are the only voice talent with whom the client is doing business. They likely won't know what they are paying for if your invoice just reads "voiceover services." Clients will not track you down for invoice corrections. They will however, fail to pay the bill if they don't know what it is for.

It's never a bad idea to keep a paper back-up of jobs you have done. Print your invoice, the script and any additional paperwork related to the job and back up or print any emails too - especially the email that authorized the work. You never want a client to be able to dispute the authorization or approval of your VO work. Use a small filing cabinet to track and store this info. Should a dispute arise and a client refuses to pay, you will have everything you need to prove that they do in fact owe you money.

*If your client authorized a job over the phone, ask them to send you an email recapping the phone call. You might also send them a recap in an email and ask them to approve or okay it. Doing so will get you the documentation you need for your billing records.

On the next page is a sample invoice that you may use to better understand all of the necessary information your invoices should contain.

Bill to:

Awesome Client
123 Any Street
Anytown, CX 12345
123-456-7890

Ship to:

Me and My VO Company
456 Any Street
Anytown, CX 12345
123-456-7890

Invoice Number: VO201614
Invoice Date: January 3, 2017
Payment Due: February 2, 2017
Amount Due (USD): **$1,500.00**

Voiceover Details	Quantity	Rate	Amount
Narration 2 minute corporate documentary VO for project titled: Our Story	1	$1,500.00	$1,500.00

Total: $1,500.00

Amount Due (USD): **$1,500.00**

Collections

Collections are a necessary part of business. Sadly, all business owners must be prepared for the possibility of having to track down, hound and harass clients in order to be paid for work performed and previously invoiced.

It is unwise to enter into ANY service-oriented business and assume you will always be paid on time. I recommend that you have collection policies, procedures and forms ready to go before a collection problem arises.

Whenever a client is late to pay an invoice - based on your company's outlined policies – their account will go into a state of collection. Some clients are slow to pay and some, for whatever reason, might refuse to pay you. If you have not been paid in:

30 days, it is customary to send a reminder email or letter to your client reminding them of your payment terms and asking for payment.

60 days, you should send a second, slightly more forceful request for payment.

90 days, you should send a third request for immediate payment that includes a deadline. If payment is not received by this deadline, you will terminate your service to the client and their account will be closed and turned over to a collection agency.

Each letter should be cordial but firm in the attempt to collect a debt. If you've never seen a collection letter, search for sample versions on the internet.

If you still have not received payment after three notices, you may want to send the client's invoice to a collection agency. Collection agencies will usually charge a fee of 20% for all money they collect. It's best to use them only as a last resort and if there is a large sum involved.

After six months of attempting to collect a debt, you will need to make a decision. Either turn the account over to an attorney or write it off as bad debt on your taxes. Writing it off is usually the better option as further collection attempts will only cost you more time and money. You've lost enough of both by this time.

If your day-to-day billing system is in order, then collections can be a very easy process. Most talent waste time with collections because they are not prepared to collect late payments. Have a clear policy – in writing - regarding clients who fail to pay in a timely manner and enforce that policy strictly.

This policy should be available on your website, invoices or by request. Make sure that all new clients receive a copy of this policy along with their first invoice. You may even want to ask them to sign and fax it back to you as a way of acknowledging that they received it.

A typical policy might state:

All first-time clients are expected to pay in advance of first voiceover. After first successful payment, you will automatically have a 30-day credit system to use for placing future voiceover orders. Future jobs must be paid within 30 days of the date of the job. If your account should become more than 90 days delinquent the said account will be shut down and all voiceover work will be suspended. Should you bring your account to good standing after a 90-day delinquency; all credit privileges will remain revoked. Should you wish to reinstate recording privileges; all future jobs will require payment-in-full, in advance.

Set aside a little time each month to review all the outstanding accounts in your billing system. Move systematically through the 30-, 60- and 90-day past-due accounts, in order.

Sample of 30-Days Past Due Notice

Your Company Name
Address and Logo   Date:
[Recipient's Name]
[Title]
[Company Name]
[Street Address] [City State, Zip code]

Dear [Recipient's Name],
Our records show that payment for invoice #### is now 30 days past due. Perhaps you forgot or even misplaced your last statement.

Please accept this reminder that payment is now due. If your check has already been sent, please disregard this notice. Thank you for your cooperation.

Sincerely,

[Your name, title, phone and email]

Sample of 60-Days Past Due Notice

Your Company Name
Address and Logo   Date:
[Recipient's Name]
[Title]
[Company Name]
[Street Address] [City State, Zip code]

Dear [Recipient's Name],

Our records show that payment for invoice #### is now 60 days past due. Perhaps you forgot or even misplaced your last statement.

We've enclosed a copy of the invoice for your convenience. Your account is in jeopardy of being closed. Please treat this matter with prompt attention. If your check has already been sent, you may disregard this notice. Thank you for your cooperation.

Sincerely,

[Your name, title, phone and email]

Sample of 90-days Past Due Notice

Your Company Name
Address and Logo   Date:
[Recipient's Name]
[Title]
[Company Name]
[Street Address] [City State, Zip code]

Dear [Recipient's Name],
Our records show that payment for invoice #### for a total of ($$$) is now more than 90 days past due. We have sent you two prior requests for payment and still have not received the amount shown above.
We have several options that will allow you to get this payment to us within the next 5 business days. They include: (list options for payment).
If no payment is received by [5 days from this letter], the following actions will take place:

1. Your account will be closed and all business, pending and future will be canceled.
2. A standard submission to the Better Business Bureau will be filed.
3. A collection agency will be assigned to this account in an effort to collect funds on our behalf.
4. Possible legal action will commence in an attempt to recover owed funds.

Please contact me upon receipt of this letter at [your phone number] so that we may discuss how to resolve this matter quickly.

Sincerely,
[Your name, title, phone and email]

Tax Deductions

As an independent business owner, you can deduct business expenses from your taxes each year. It is wise to save and track receipts in categories based on the type of expense they are. While I am not an accountant (I recommend you consult a tax advisor/CPA), most VO talent successfully deduct the following expenses:

- A portion of your rent or mortgage - for the business use of your home. The percentage you may deduct is based on the square footage of your office and home studio/office. If your home is 1,000 square feet and your office is 200 square feet; your business use of home is 20%. This means you can deduct 20% of your rent or mortgage and other home related expenses. However this space must be 100% dedicated to business use in order for you to expense it.

- Your business-related utilities such as electricity, water, phone, cell phone, internet, ISDN, etc.

- Computer equipment and software including equipment repairs.

- Office furniture and office supplies.

- Marketing materials (including your demos) and any purchased advertising.

- Voiceover lessons, seminars and training.

- Travel expenses related to business, such as hotels and meals.

- Car payments, fuel, mileage and repairs – for a vehicle used for business.
- Entertainment and dining expenses for business-related affairs.

- Postage and shipping costs related to business.
- Memberships, dues and fees related to industry clubs and organizations.
- Gifts valued at less than $25 that you purchase for clients.
- Vendors or outsourced employees that you hire to perform work for you.
- Medical, dental and vision expenses OR self-employed health insurance premiums.
- Charitable donations made by the company to a qualified not-for-profit company.

A deductible expense, according to the IRS must be ordinary and necessary for you to conduct business. It must also be reasonable. If you need to purchase something to make money, it is a business expense.

The following items cannot be deducted from your taxes:

- Grocery items unrelated to your business.
- Furniture that is not related to your office.
- Travel expenses unrelated to your business.
- Gifts for your family and friends.
- Utilities unrelated to business/utilities for personal use.
- Recreational expenses.

You must allocate percentages of items that you share between your home and your business. This can include most utilities.

> Tax laws change frequently. It is best to work with a CPA or - use the IRS's website (www.IRS.gov), year to year, in order to keep track of items that are deductible and those that are not.

Chapter 3
Daily Operations

Contact Management

Be diligent with your records every single day. Contact management can be cumbersome but as little as 15 minutes per day can make it a regular and easy process. Since out-of-sight means out-of-mind, you must be able to easily and quickly access your business contacts and communicate with them. Retain as much information as you can about a person. House and save a contact's:

- Name
- Office Phone / Cell Phone
- Email
- Website Address
- Mailing Address
- Business Type
- Date you last spoke

> There are many great products for tracking your business contacts. "ACT!" is a software used by salespeople to track jobs, prospects, clients and leads.
>
> "Outlook" and "Plaxo" offer software and online contact management solutions, too.
>
> "Performer Track" is specially designed to address the specific needs of performers and is the product I recommend most to VO talent.

Track and record info even if you think you don't need it. If you don't do this, you will prevent yourself from using or having future forms of marketing. That's not a situation in which you want to be.

Many VO talent do not keep the mailing addresses of potential clients because they use email as their primary means of communication. That's fine, until one day you decide that you want to send a postcard to everyone on your contact list. NOW you have the monstrous task of procuring all those addresses.

It is also wise to record a note section with your contact records so that you won't struggle to remember who someone is or what you last spoke about. It's never a bad idea to record spouse or children's names and other small personal details about a client or prospective client. These details allow you to be personal and friendly with each and every person with whom you communicate.

Be sure that you can notate, flag, sort or color-code records for follow-up purposes. You want to make certain that you have an at-a-glance view of whom to follow up with and when. This ensures that you never forget to follow up with someone. When setting up a contact management system, it's best to implement a way to track contacts by type and industry too. This will let you quickly and efficiently sort and separate advertising agencies, production houses, video producers and industry-specific clients such as audio book publishers or promo producers at television stations and networks.

Make certain that addresses are also searchable separately, by city and zip code. This can be very handy when doing market research later or if you happen to travel to a particular city and want to set up some meetings.

Set aside a dedicated time every day for the purpose of contact management entry and follow-up. By permanently scheduling an hour a week or 15 minutes per day, you ensure that your contacts are up-to-date, well organized and ready to use for marketing, advertising and prospecting.

It's also a good idea to make certain that your contact management system integrates with your billing system. Certain billing systems can double as contact management tools. At the very least if you are using two separate software systems, one for billing and one for contact management, make sure they are able to communicate with one another.

Lastly, you'll probably want to set aside time monthly or quarterly for the larger contact management task known as prospecting. Prospecting (finding new people to reach out to and offer your services) can be a tedious process but it's essential to the development of your business and its continued growth.

Outsourcing

As your client roster grows you might want to consider outsourcing tasks like collections, billing and all other account receivable payable processes. Outsourcing can equal big benefits for voiceover talent.

Outsourcing a job means that you are transferring it to an off-site person or external company to manage and conduct. This can provide you with needed additional man-power and allows you to experience greater productivity for a lot less than it would cost to hire a full-time or part-time employee.

Domestic outsourcing is common. Technically, the clients that you work for "outsource" their VO needs. So what can you outsource? It's very possible that outsourcing might save you time and money where you need help. One of its biggest benefits is redirecting tasks that you dislike or aren't very proficient in.

Billing, collections, business prospecting, social network management, marketing, public relations and even audio production can all be outsourced to capable off-site personnel. You may benefit greatly from a simple shift in your business model, especially if you are struggling to accomplish everything.

You can find qualified professionals by using staffing companies that specialize in outsourcing but the options they offer will likely be pricey and possibly even restrictive for your needs. Your best bet is to use friends, word of mouth, Craig's List and local colleges or universities to find qualified applicants.

Much of the work you need performed can be done outside of

regular business hours, so you might be able to find someone interested in making a little side money for less than their full rate.

Outsourcing is easily managed by establishing a set agreement with the person you hire. Decide on a number of hours of work per week or month for a price you both like. Make sure that you have a way to manage their progress and see the benefits of their work.

Outsourcing is also fantastic because it allows you to have people working for you without invading your space and if you work from home like most talent, you know how important space can be! In addition, your "employee" becomes responsible for their own resources in order to conduct business. They must supply their own phone lines, Internet access, computer, supplies, etc.

If you choose to seek external assistance for things like billing and collections; the stress relief you receive alone may be worth the money.

If you're handling these tasks yourself, you know how difficult it can be repeatedly asking for money from a client or business associate. It can be difficult to remain emotionless if clients become a hassle when it comes to getting paid. Your outsourced person will likely remain calm and cool and will also allow you to sound like a larger, better-managed company.

If your studio time is saturated and you're finding it very difficult to properly edit and prepare auditions and bookings, you may want to seek out an audio producer who is readily available and will quickly, cleanly and seamlessly prepare your auditions and final jobs.

An alternative to outsourcing is to begin a small internship or apprentice program. There are many talented individuals who are just begging to get a voiceover career started.

Assuming that your VO career is already underway and that you're making some money from bookings, interns are a way to get no or low cost labor in exchange for your time and expertise. Internships.com is a great resource, as are local colleges and universities. A qualified student can be put to specific tasks and they learn by watching you in action, as well as being given tasks and goals.

> **VO Edit by Design** specializes in the editing needs of VO talent at affordable rates.
>
> Contact owner Chris Thomas by visiting:
> www.VOEditByDesign.com

Notes: *Use the space below to write notes, questions or reminders related to outsourcing services, internships and companies that may benefit you now or in the future.*

_____
_____
_____
_____
_____
_____
_____
_____

Contracts

There are a variety of types of VO work that require a contract. It behooves you to have a contact established long before the need for one actually arises. Radio Imaging, TV Promo, IVR work, any recurring job and occasionally commercial work may require a contractual agreement between you and a client.

It is always in your best interest to present your own contract rather than have the client provide one for you to sign. One the next page, I've typed out a standard retainer contract that you may use anytime the need for a contract arises. Simply fill in the blanks for your specific situation. A contract like the one to follow can be modified for use in monthly, quarterly, yearly or even one-time-use situations.

Talent Name

c/o YOUR COMPANY NAME
123 Smith Street, Any-Town, USA, 01234
Voiceover Contract: Client Name, Any-Town, USA

YOUR NAME, (hereinafter referred to as "Talent") agrees to provide (name the type of work and be very specific) for the benefit of WXX /Any- Town, USA (hereinafter referred to as "Client") located at 1000 Some Street, Some Town, ST 01234. Talent agrees that this on-air radio material is exclusive to client and will not be available to any other (name the type of business) in the market Any-Town, USA.

Talent shall provide Client (name the monthly term of material you will provide) per month. Additional pages above the term are available for purchase at a rate of $000.00 per page. Talent will be unavailable to record 4 weeks per year which may or may not be consecutive. A minimum of a 72-hour notice will be given to client. Talent will be unavailable to record on any holiday upon which the banks, stock market, and U.S. Post Office are closed. Audio can be sent via MP3 or via the carrier of client's choice, with freight billed to client. Client can also have tracks sent "real time" via ISDN data lines with such fees paid by Client.

Client's use of the (name the material being provided) as provided under this agreement, shall extend only for the length of this Agreement. Client shall hold Talent harmless and indemnify Talent from any damage or liability resulting from any voiced message recorded by Talent on behalf of Client. Client agrees to pay on a "pay or play" basis the sum of ($0,000) for a period of one year. Payment in this term will be Client's option of either all $0,000 up front or payments of ($000) each month with payment due PRIOR to the start of each month. The first month of $000.00 (due by 00/00/00) and all subsequent payments is made payable to YOUR NAME, YOUR ADDRESS.

Additional voiceover usage for other projects and presentations for Client will be an extra charge negotiated in good faith. The term of this Agreement shall begin on the 1st day of January 2020 and end the last day of December 2020. Client may not use any performances recorded by Talent in any manner after the term, nor may they be resold in whole or in part at any time. Either party may cancel this agreement with SIXTY (60) days written notice received (no pro-rated months if canceled). Additional years will automatically renew at the start of the new term at the same terms plus TEN (10) percent compensation.

This Agreement represents our complete understanding and may not be assigned without the written consent of both parties. This Agreement shall be construed by and interpreted in accordance with the laws and judicial decisions of the State of YOUR STATE.

_____ (talent) _____ (date)

_____ (Official officer of client)

_____ (date)

Budgeting For Success

Lots of talent are looking for work, but have no advertising or marketing budget set aside to work with. This is the proverbial catch-22. "I need money to make money, and I have none, so I'm stuck." Is this you? It doesn't have to be. You can easily change your situation with some better decision making, record keeping and planning. Every business needs an advertising budget and VO is no exception. You shouldn't be in business without one!

First up, choose to make better decisions. Far too often, talent invest their money in the wrong places. They spend thousands of dollars on microphones, high-end computers and other studio gadgets, then are left with no money for advertising or marketing - the very thing that is going to help put all that equipment to use. High-end equipment is not worth the expense if your business can't justify the purchase.

If you're just starting out as a voice talent, you might be tempted to buy high-end equipment thinking that it is going to help you book more work. Bad move. It's not necessary to spend mega bucks on a studio when you can find great deals on E-bay and a plethora of lower-cost items for recording and soundproofing. You'll get a better return on your investment by working with a coach, having a new demo made, or building a website.

Before making any purchase, ask yourself, "Is this going to help me book more work?" If the answer is "no" or "maybe", look for a better option. Make sure that you can justify each and every purchase you make. Do not allow personal wants to over-shadow needs, especially if those needs can be met with a thrifty alternative.

Next up is record keeping. Plan to make 3 quarterly investments in the next year towards marketing and advertising. The way to do this is simple. Have a separate bank account set up just for marketing. Most talent have a personal savings account. You can use this or open a business savings account. Allocate 5-10 % of all your voiceover earnings into your marketing fund.

If you are just starting out in VO and your VO earnings are none existent but you have other income, you may need to allocate 5-10 % of your day-job earnings to make this happen.

Okay now here's the catch. As soon as you get paid, transfer the money out of your checking account into the marketing account. If you have trouble remembering to do this or just sticking to the plan, talk to your bank. Most banks can set up your accounts so that these transactions take place automatically. It will take some adjusting at first but after a month or two you will not miss the income that is being set aside.

At the end of each quarter, make purchases from your Wish List (coming up in the next section of this book) and update your list to reevaluate priorities.

As you gain more jobs, you will have more to spend each quarter. You can reinvest and grow your overall exposure each quarter with the products that work best for you as well as trying out new ones. You most likely won't see results from your marketing for about 3-6 months, so be sure to give your purchases time to work before you decide something is a waste of time.

Chapter 4
Branding & Marketing

Increasing Profits with Marketing and Sales

Marketing and Advertising are an essential part of business. Without them, potential clients won't know what you offer. If they don't know what makes your voice unique or how to find you, your business can stagnate.

Marketing/Advertising are also typically the most expensive services you will need for your business, but they don't have to be. Effective marketing takes strategy and planning.

The first thing you will need is a list of potential clients that hire VO talent. You can start building this list on your own by researching client/agency websites, cold calling and by attending industry events. You will need to keep track of everyone you talk to by entering them into a database as discussed in the section "Contact Management".

> There are several companies (including Radio Mall, Sales Leads USA, Ad Base & more) that will sell you lists of names for specific industries.

In order to build your database, there are several proven techniques that will help you gain contacts. The first is to scour the Internet for any and all relevant websites or companies that typically hire voice talent. Advertising agencies, production companies, animation studios, video editors and producers, all have VO needs.

In addition, use services and websites like Production Hub, Call Sheet /Backstage, Mandy.com, Showbiz Weekly as well as any industry-specific trade publications and websites related to the industries you are trying to reach.

Almost all professional organizations have some form of online or print material. Radio imaging, TV Promo, telephony and audio book voiceovers all correspond to an industry. Find the "insider" websites and magazines used by the industry you are targeting.

Make it a point to get out and meet people. VO can be a very isolated industry if you allow it to be. Your business can't thrive if no one knows about you. So go to local business owner meetings and network events. You can find many in your area at Meetup.com.

When you attend these events, your goal should be to collect as many cards from potential sources of work as you can. You don't want the contact info of other talent. It's not to say you should be rude or unwilling to make friends with other voiceover talent. You must be aware that other actors can help you improve your skills as a performer, but they will not generally help you find work and grow your business. You don't want to become a voice talent that markets to other voice talent.

I've helped many talent over the years to become aware of this error and make the necessary steps to correct the problem. It's wonderful to have friends in any industry, but unless your goal is to become a coach or a service provider to other voiceover actors, having hundreds of them in your contacts won't help you very much.

Once you have your client lists built, you can start sending out direct mail pieces with your website information; emailing your demo, or cold calling and introducing yourself. Ideally, you should be applying all of these in some manner during your work week.

> You can & should have a website. Use it to house your demos & visually present the sound of your voice. SnapPages & Wix.com offer DIY websites at VERY affordable prices.
> Or hire a pro to help you create one.

You can place ads on industry websites too. You can have an email blast, a newsletter or send a CD of your demo to your entire contact list. All of these are proven methods of advertising. You should take advantage of all that you can afford!

Please don't view this all-important process as one enormous task. Marketing and advertising may be complex at times but they are best managed in small sections that are broken down into yearly, quarterly, monthly or even weekly goals. Before you spend a single cent on anything you need to research all of the potential marketing and advertising options that are available to you.

This process should not be difficult. Reputable companies will have clear, easy-to-read options on their websites. A single call or email should clarify any questions that you have. And companies should be willing to send you additional supporting information of the claims they make. All advertising companies, especially those in print and web offer rate cards – just ask for those.

Multimedia companies and marketing consultants who offer many solutions to common problems should be willing to create a customized action plan for you, including cost estimates. Gather everything you've gleaned from all sources and put it in a spreadsheet. You want to define the company who offers the product or service, specifications (such as what you will receive or the size of an ad) and of course, cost. This will be especially helpful with SEO and online visibility companies like Google and Yelp that try to help you market your website. Even Pay to Play websites like Voice123 and Voices.com should be part of this list.

You'll update this list anytime you think of something new that your business needs or whenever an offer comes to you that looks interesting. From here on out, we're going to refer to this list as the Wish List.

Prioritize the Wish List. You may color code entries or number them. Whatever you choose; the idea is to better understand what marketing items are critical, which are important and which can wait. About once a month, you should revisit the Wish List, add to it, and make sure that you still agree with the priority items.

Let's talk about paying for these items, shall we? I'm not going to ask you to rob a bank. However some strategic banking is in order. Make a decision to set aside a set percentage of your business income to marketing and advertising.

Anything from 5 to 50% will work and should be determined based on what you can afford and how new you are to voiceovers. New-comers should expect to put near 100% of their VO earnings back into their VO career. Allocate your chosen percentage to a marketing fund.

Once you have enough money, go ahead and purchase your first priority item from the Wish List. As time goes by, you'll be able to move through the list and accomplish your marketing goals more easily and steadily. The best part is you won't have to spend money out-of-pocket to do it.

Marketing & Promotions Wish List			
Priority	Item	Details	Cost

Promotions, Branding and Marketing

How potential customers see and view your name and services is a large part of your success. There are whole sections of book-stores dedicated to helping you promote and brand your business.

Whenever a company or executive comes up with a new brand concept, everyone wants to know what it is and how they did it. Most are willing to share this vital information. However their methods may not work for everyone. However the "Three Commandments of Marketing" are essential to any successful campaign. They are:

> Know Thy Services
> Know Thy Customers
> Know Thy Competition

Repeatedly ask yourself:

a) What does my name, brand, company (my voice) sound / look like?

b) How do I communicate those ideas quickly and easily to potential clients?

c) What is important to a potential client and how do I appeal to them?

d) How can I reach the largest number of potential clients and spend the least amount of time/money doing it?

e)   What is my competition doing?

Your answers to these questions will change from year to year and may become more complex over time. As you start to find a niche for yourself in the voice industry, you may also need to streamline these questions to the specific types of clients for whom you work.

This is not beginner information either. It is the same process I recommend to established VO talent. The goal is to avoid becoming "the best talent no one has ever heard of." Branding and marketing help you to be a public company.

Current Answers to KEY Marketing Questions: *Use the space below to answer the questions asked on the previous page. Periodically review your answers and update them. Make sure you notate the date of each entry.*

_____
_____
_____
_____
_____
_____
_____
_____
_____
_____
_____
_____
_____
_____
_____

Marketing Misconceptions

Many voiceover actors make the mistake of thinking that the look of their marketing material doesn't matter all that much. This is not only incorrect, it's potentially very damaging to your business.

Your primary branding tools are your demo (which hopefully you have made a significant and thoughtful investment into its creation), your physical CD demo which you'll use very sparingly nowadays, your cover letter, website, business cards and possibly postcards.

Each one should match (creating a cohesive package) and look expensive, even if they aren't. They should express your sound. And always remember that any impression could be your first impression. Agents, in particular, are bothered by two things, sloppy/poor presentation and desperation – which we will talk about in much detail later.

You are not applying for a job, or traditional employment, so don't be too stuffy or cordial. You are a business owner connecting with other business owners. You are looking to form meaningful and mutually beneficial partnerships.

Images, pictures, and graphics must help me emotionally connect with the sound of your voice along with a brand or positioning statement that is cooperative with your demo and explains quickly what you do best.

Does Your Company Look As Good As You Sound?

1. See Your Voice in Pictures

Most people absorb their world visually.

Visual stimuli are usually more memorable than sounds.

Creating an emotional connection with images can be powerful.

VO talent aren't visual creatures – we absorb our world via what we hear, whereas the general population doesn't.

> **If a picture can describe your *sound* <u>AND</u> is worth a thousand words, let your marketing images do some of the talking!**

List how each picture above makes you feel

_____   _____

_____   _____

_____   _____

_____   _____

List four adjectives that describe each of the images above

_____   _____
_____   _____
_____   _____
_____   _____

What Words Describe Your Voice?

Use the space below to list as many adjectives that you can think of that describe the sound of your voice.

_____
_____
_____

Are You an Optimist or a Pessimist?

Be true to who you are – even in your branding. Your brand is best when it's honest and gives a genuine insight into your personality as a performer. Write down a little about your world- view and your overall outlook on life.

_____
_____
_____

Describe In Your Own Words, Your Personal Style...

Just like decorating a room in your house, you have a personal sense of style and what appeals to you. Colors, texture, design, patterns, etc. Are you sleek and modern or rugged and rustic?

_____
_____
_____

2. Recognize These Images?

Which of these images is most recognized globally?
Did somebody say..."McDonalds"?

We are not saying that VO talent should strive to build a brand so powerful that it will be as well-known as the Nike swoosh, but to the clients you market to and to the industry you service, your brand should be readily recognized.

You achieve this in the same way major corporations do. Namely, with frequency and consistency. Clients should see your brand often and your brand image should have longevity. You want to be certain that with minor tweaking, updating and modernization, you brand's message will last for many decades to come. Heritage brands like McDonald's and Coca-Cola update their logo every decade or so. However the logo is still essentially the same.

If you feel your brand is too trendy or that it will "expire" soon, you may want to modify it. Being the 'Hipster Voice

Actor' might be a little too hip. Also think about your voice and how it may age. If you're brand only focuses on how you sound today, right this minute, you might create something with a short lifespan.

3. Cliché Images to Avoid:

What do any of these images say about your voice?

Without sales and marketing training, many VO talent fail to think from a buyer's perspective. If you are a VO buyer, you likely didn't just stumble upon the website of a random VO talent. You were probably looking for a talent to cast in an upcoming project. So when you go to a voiceover website and see pictures of microphones, mixing boards, sound waves and headphones, you aren't being told anything about how that individual talent sounds. The actor doesn't really have a brand if that's all they display. In fact, the only message being reiterated with those images is something the buyer already knew "I speak for a living."

A microphone does not have a sound all its own. Can you describe how a mic sounds? Microphones, audio waves, headphones, etc., do not tell us anything about how YOU sound. They are soulless and soundless until you come in.

A buyer wants help making a clear choice. The images you choose should be able to help create a strong understanding of the sound, skills and performance they can expect to receive from you. Microphones and sound waves don't accomplish this.

Look at promotional pictures of current recording artists. The recording industry spends millions branding their artists. A CD's cover will give you an indication of the type of music you can expect. Likewise, photo shoots are staged to help the artist have an outward appearance that well represents both the genre of music they offer and a fan's expectations.

In other words, a rock band looks like a rock band and an R&B singer looks like an R&B singer and so on. The audience can identify which recording artist will likely appeal to them just by the way the artist is presented and potentially never having heard their music.

The music industry understands and embraces branding. It takes a lot of work to become KISS, Lady Gaga, Mariah Carey, Beyoncé, etc. There's a tremendous amount of effort that goes into building a musical brand and using that brand to connect to a fan base. Voiceover actors are trying to do the same thing, only with a smaller audience made up almost entirely of voiceover buyers.

Another industry that 'gets' entertainment branding is wrestling. I see you snickering. Seriously, the WWE is a company founded on marketing masterminds. Wrestlers all have a unique persona that helps brand them as a hero or a villain and audiences can't get enough.

4. Should I Show My Face?

Using only a few words, describe how each person sounds:

_____
_____
_____

Now I'm asking you to do something you've been taught NEVER to do. I am asking you to judge a book by its cover. Please stereotype and make generalizations about the people in these images.

In the movie "Up in the Air", George Clooney's character says, "I always stereotype; it's faster."

> **How we look does affect how others expect us to sound. If you don't sound the way you look (or vice versa), it's not a good idea to use a photo to market yourself.**

It's human nature to pass judgment. The same way YOU judge something based on what you see, your client will too. They may determine if you are the right voice for their job based on how you look, not how you sound. Your physical characteristics should not be a factor in the VO work you book. And they won't be, unless you choose to include a photo in your marketing.

==DO use your photo if it represents your brand well and has the potential to enforce your brand message. DON'T use a photo if you sound completely different that you look.==

How would you "judge" these real actor headshots?

Age is an important thing to consider when showing your face. Do you sound younger or older than you look? You will shatter the audience's illusion of how you look the moment you show them. This can lead to type-casting.

Years ago I did a blind study to determine the results of how casting directors are influenced by what they see and how a picture will affect what they hear. Here is what my staff and I did:

We first submitted a dozen demos to a casting director looking to hire a female voice actress "in her 20s". The women we submitted ranged in age from 30 to 50. Only two were rejected for sounding too old. The top pick for the casting was actually a woman of 45 who has a notably young sound.

We then had another person in our office submit a second round of submissions. This time each demo came along with a headshot or photo of each actress. Once again, they ranged in age from 30- 50 and where being submitted for a 20-something casting. All but a scant few were rejected for sounding too old or "not right" for the project. None from this group where included in the final selection.

We replicated this months later with a male group. Same results. And there are some excellent "20-something" male voiceover actors that are actually men in their late 40's and early 50's, who just happen to sound very young. Normally they receive consideration without a problem. But when we included a photo, the decisions makers where immediately influenced by what they saw – mainly gray hair.

5. The Use of Color

Colors are a form of non-verbal communication.

You must understand how the eye and mind perceive colors and their meanings. Make no mistake, every color has a meaning. Each color represents an emotion or an idea to the person viewing it. Color is a very powerful mood changer and enhancer. There's a reason why gray, rainy days make us depressed and sunny bright days make us happy.

Colors follow trends. Hunter green, for instance, is a more masculine, intelligent color. On the other hand, sea foam green is a feminine, more caring color and avocado green was a popular appliance color in the 1970s. I still have flashbacks of my parent's refrigerator.

All colors have three sides – based on hue:
Strong or Soft   Bold or Light   Electric or Subdued

> **Don't pick a color simply because you like it.
> Choose colors that wil represent the sound of your voice.**

So, What Colors Are Your Voice?

_____
_____
_____
_____
_____
_____

Color Psychology

Use this info to find the best colors for your voice:

Black - Black is the color of authority and power. It is stylish, timeless, sophisticated and sexy. It can be overpowering; perceived as evil, villainous or even harsh. Black can be serious and conventional, too.

White - White is the color of innocence and purity. White reflects light. Since it is light and neutral, it goes with everything. Doctors and nurses wear white to imply sterility.

Red - The most emotionally intense color. Red stimulates a faster heartbeat and breathing. It is also the color of love. Red can also mean anger or it can be a caution or warning. Red is hot.

Pink - The most romantic color. Pink is soft, sweet, delicate and feminine. It is friendly and inviting.

Blue - Blue is one of the most popular colors. It causes the opposite reaction as red. Peaceful and tranquil, blue causes the body to produce calming chemicals. Blue symbolizes loyalty, importance and confidence. Dark blue, often considered a "corporate color" is associated with intelligence, stability and conservatism.

Green - Always a popular decorating color. Green symbolizes nature, life, renewal and intellect. It is the easiest color on the eye. It is calming, refreshing and symbolizes fertility. Dark green is masculine, conservative and implies wealth.

Yellow - Cheerful sunny yellow is an attention getter and is considered an optimistic color. It is the most difficult color for the eye to take in, so it can be overpowering if overused.

Purple - The color of royalty. Purple symbolizes creativity, imagination, luxury and wealth. It is also feminine and romantic. However, because it is rare in nature, purple can appear artificial.

Brown - Solid, reliable and dependable - that's brown! Light brown implies genuineness while dark brown is wholesome, simple and friendly. Many men say brown is one of their favorite colors.

Orange - Orange is stimulating and is often associated with change. It can be found in fall leaves and in the setting sun. It is both an edgy and sophisticated color.

Notes:
Use the space below to write notes, questions or reminders related to colors that might be a good fit for your voiceover marketing and branding.

_____
_____
_____
_____
_____
_____
_____
_____
_____
_____

6. Analyzing your Sound - Find Your Look

Subjective Vocal Attributes	Objective Vocal Attributes
Write down subjective emotions, feelings and ideas about your voice.	Write down objective, concrete, tangible images that represent your voice.
1. 2. 3. 4. 5. 6. 7. 8. 9. 10.	1. 2. 3. 4. 5. 6. 7. 8. 9. 10.
Ask friends, family, and colleagues to participate in this process. Play your demo and ask them:	
"How does my voice make you feel?"	**"What place or thing does my voice remind you of?"**

Also ask: What color Am I?

Does my voice remind you of a celebrity or notable person?

Use contact lists, Facebook and other social network sites to receive feedback from your focus group. Then, denote any similar words, phrases or ideas and group them together in a spreadsheet. This exercise may yield your exact marketing plan or it may be a launching pad that leads to other ideas. I have yet to see it fail in the hands of a creative individual.

7. Working with Graphic and Web Designers

When working with a graphic or web designer, there are a few steps you should take to ensure the best experience possible.

1.   Discuss cliché images you want to avoid, such as the microphones, headphones, mixing boards, and others listed earlier in this chapter.

2.   Talk with your designer about the "feel" of the images you want to use and the over-all message the design should convey. Use your subjective and objective columns to better prepare them with feedback and ideas.   3.   Use the Sound Analysis sheet to help your designer understand how the public perceives you. Your designer can then make suggestions on how to enhance positive perceptions and decrease negatives.

4.   Discuss all possible future mediums for which your design will be used. Such as print, web, CD cases, etc. Make certain to request master files of the artwork in a variety of sizes and file types.

5.   Never accept a logo with an unchangeable or static background color, as this will make future changes VERY difficult. A Photoshop PNG file should ensure that you have a transparent design option for future use.

6.   Obtain three possible design proofs/options. Use those proposed designs to help narrow down things you like and things you don't.

7.   Proceed with all plans as if your designer will vanish and never be heard from within two weeks of the project's

completion. It happens all the time! Designers simply vanish. This can make for tragic and highly frustrating business roadblocks later. It's best to assume you'll never work with this person again and get everything you need from them ASAP.

8.   Plan and map your website's content and functions before any design work begins. In fact, if a website is part of the design plan, everything else (business cards, logo, print designs in- general) should revolve around the creation of the website. This way all graphics will be cohesive and orderly. Not all graphic artists are website designers and not all website creators are great graphic artists.

9.   Discuss website expansions and create a solid platform for future changes. There's nothing more frustrating than finding out your site has to be rebuilt or significantly changed to accommodate a request later. This is both costly and time consuming and can be avoided with a little additional planning.

10.   Try to obtain a final website that is not dependent on the designer for minor changes and revisions. Ideally the site will be yours and you will own it after it's complete. You'll be able to access its text and design features and make updates whenever you like. Your designer's only long-term agenda should be hosting or nothing at all. Wix.com, SnapPages, and even WordPress allow you to work with a designer to create the look and feel of the site and then leave you to your own devices to complete the remainder.

11.   Remind your designer that the website you own should be 100% about marketing your voice, not about website bells and whistles. Never hire a designer that is too technical and offers little knowledge or assistance with branding.

Branding When I'm Brand New

When you start looking at the branding, marketing and websites of existing voiceover actors, you can become discouraged very easily. It seems like everyone has more experience. Each actor has an extensive list of clients and Fortune 500 names, along with a resume of credits.

But soon, you'll realize that even very, very, new voiceover actors have a client list. How can this be? How are they so lucky? They aren't. They are simply 'faking it, until they make it."

Brand new talent must take a look at their previous work history and experience. What name brand companies have you worked for? Did you work at a fast food joint in high school or college? Did you have a retail job at some point? Were you ever a server at a well-known chain restaurant? Do you volunteer or fundraise with a national charity? Meet your clients! If they can appear on a standard, traditional resume as work experience, then they are valid, temporary additions to your voiceover client list.

You'll want to replace these names with real voiceover clients as soon as possible. For the time being, they will give you a boost of confidence and something to show for yourself in the way of experience. Do clients ever 'check-on' or ask about these past clients. Nope. They take your word for it.

Use the space below to write down all the name-brand companies or affiliated companies you have worked for or with.

_____

_____

_____

Do It Yourself Marketing

Voice talent must begin to learn what school-teachers and Martha Stewart have known for years, that a little creativity can make magic. Do-it-yourself projects can really be effective for marketing. Plan well and decide on a budget. Spending just $100 can sometimes look like you spent $1000.

Business Cards

VistaPrint.com is one of the cheapest and fastest ways to obtain cards. Sign up to receive their email offers because they run a slew of sales, non-stop. You should never pay full price for a Vista-Print product.

Never use a Vista-Print template "as is"! The templates seem cool until you realize that every ready-made design (especially those with a microphone) are being used by thousands of other voice talent. Modify templates by swapping photos, images, colors and fonts. Customized cards have more impact.

Vista Print and their small quantity orders are hard to find elsewhere; that makes their prices rather attractive. However, when it comes to large print jobs (anything over 500), Vista Print is actually overpriced. At GotPrint.com you can order 1000 business cards for as little as $8.00! Shop around.

Magazines

Spend a few hours at your local book-store with a cup of coffee and review all the latest craft magazines. You will get dozens of great ideas (including seasonal ones) to help you market and promote your brand. If you're handy with a glue gun and don't mind putting in some evening hours, you can really add a unique and personal touch to your marketing. You can create your own thank you cards, CD cases and more.

Craft Stores

Likewise, wander around the craft store and see what you find. There are kits of all kinds! Make drink coasters, holiday ornaments, pencil holders, magnets and more with your business name, logo and look. You'll even find stickers, stamps, appliqués and scrapbooking supplies that can help you create a signature brand. Plus, stickers and stamps instantly customize anything you put them on.

Oriental Trading

Oriental Trading is a bulk supplier of party items that are all categorized by theme. There are thousands of products geared for every age and taste and they are super cheap! Toys, gift-bag items, party favors galore – most of which can easily be used as a small business "for-get-me-not" with minor customization.

M&Ms

Create your own M&M candy bags. Buy bulk bags and then repackage the candy in your own containers or bags for much less than the cost of the pre-packaged versions.

Websites

A quality, great looking website for less than $15? Yup! There are web solutions that allow you easy maintenance and control of your site without being web designer dependent. Check out SnapPages & WIX.com. Each allows you the ability to have total web control for a fraction of the cost of hiring a web development company. However, I recommend the help of a graphic designer to take the customization of these sites to the next level.

More on Websites

Do you really need a website? The answer is unequivocally, yes. Websites serve two main purposes. Your site allows you to quickly and easily be found on the internet. Your presence online is a way for your customers and potential agents or partners to verify your expertise and that you are who you say you are. Your business isn't real unless it's online. Likewise, people love to cyber stalk others in order to determine if they are in fact someone worth working with. It's the new norm. If you're trying to legitimize someone's claim, you take to Google.

If a website is built well it also brings business to you. Your site acts as not just an online calling-card, it also allows customers to find their way to you and hire you. This is the ultimate goal for a site owner. It's not just enough to have a website – you want to monetize that site and make sure it's working for you round the clock by helping potential buyers find you directly.

If you're not very web savvy, you'll need partners and help in the creation of your website. However if you're not computer shy you may want to try your hand at building and maintaining your own site – at least at first. Whether you go it alone or with help, these are the essentials to creating a website that gets results.

First you'll need a URL or Domain name. It's wise to purchase multiple domains for the same website. They can all "point" to the same location/website. It's also a good idea to purchase domains with various spellings, especially if there are elements of your domain that can be easily misspelled. Be sure to purchase both the correct and incorrect spelling. Make sure your domain is catchy, quick and easy to remember. Use the (dot).com extension whenever possible. (dot).net, (dot).me, (dot).us and the like, really aren't all that valuable.

Research a domain at Whois.net – this allows you to see what URLs are available for purchase, if they are unavailable and how active those sites are. It may take you two or three tries to find the right URL or one that is available. Now it's time to purchase your domain(s).

When purchasing your domain it's wise to purchase more than one year at a time. Search engines like Google find websites to be more credible when you purchase multiple years. It proves you're "in it" for the long haul. You can purchase your domain(s) yourself at several domain websites like: GoDaddy.com, Register.com or Networksolutions.com. Don't buy a bunch of extra stuff – don't be tempted to purchase a lot of add-on items. For now, just purchase your domain – even if you aren't ready to build a website just yet, you are securing that the address you want on the web will be available when you're ready. It's a bit like buying a plot of land and planning to develop a house on it later.

If you're going the do-it-your-self route to create your website's content, now is the time to check out Wix.com, SnapPages.com, Adobe Muse or WordPress. These DIY tools are affordable and give you complete control over the design and content of your site. You don't need to be a coding or HTML specialist either. Refer to the marketing section of this book for specifics on how to create your site and the guidelines you should follow.

Remember that content is king on the web. A very small site made up of only one page will do very little to help you be found by on the web. It's wise to create a 3 to 5 page site.

Make sure that each page contains a good balance of pictures, design elements and text. Text is critical. Ultimately text is the only thing that helps search engines to "crawl" or search your information. That text must be unique to your site and should not overwhelm the reader. There's a fine balance you must find.

Think about your site's long-term usability and the features and functions you want it to have, especially if you are working with a third party to create it. Make sure you discuss expansion and compatibility for the future. For instance, you might not think you need video content and functionality on your site right now. But if you decide in a year to add videos and you're site isn't built to support it, your designer may have to recreate all or large parts of the site and that can become very expensive.

Who will maintain your site after it's complete? You? Your designer? Make sure you have a solid plan. When you want to make changes to your site you'll want to make today, not 10 days from now. It's very important to know what to expect and to discuss what classifies as a simple, minor or major change to your designer.

Once you're site is built (or while it's being built) you'll want to research and learn as much as you can about SEO (search engine optimization) and Google Analytics. All websites can be tracked based on a variety of statistical date. Who visited, when, for how long, how did they find the site, what key words did they search, did they link to the site from somewhere else. All this and more can be analyzed to help you better understand how to put your site to work. Google Analytics is the gold standard for this process and it's free. However, I will warn you; this is a trip down the rabbit hole.

For those who are looking to really be in control of their little piece of the web, there are some amazing tools that you can master with time and patience. You can learn to integrate many, many master tricks, tools and tips to your website. Webconfs.com is an amazing resource full of SEO tools and webmaster utilities, plus a search engine simulator. Using this website will take time and patience but the education you'll receive will make you a much savvier website owner and operator.

A great website is a blend of both tech savvy techniques and marketing. Know your limits. Find the right partners and be dedicated to a learning process that will inevitably help shape your business into the future.

Use the space below to write down web related information, research, names of providers, cost of services, and your own web to-do list.

_____
_____
_____
_____
_____
_____
_____
_____
_____
_____
_____
_____
_____

Social Networking: How to Make Friends and Conduct Business

Voice talent are no strangers to the social network revolution and many talent can be found on Twitter, Facebook, Instagram and VOUniverse. If you have a profile on sites like Guru, E-lance and LinkedIn, are you taking advantage of all they have to offer your business? Are you maximizing these social sites as a business tool?

Social network sites allow you to meet clients and potential clients by reviewing their profiles and directly or indirectly starting a conversation with them about your VO services. If small business owners and entrepreneurs have such a magnificent business builder in these sites, why is it that most voice talent seem to spend time on social sites meeting other talent and little time meeting clients?

If you are using social networks, you should dedicate at least a few hours a week to finding and meeting people and updating your profile. Use the sites' search features to look up other users who are in VO-related businesses. The ones who are most likely to directly hire talent include audio and video producers, advertising executives, and marketing managers. Having a standard draft block of text ready to send to anyone you encounter will make the process even faster. Save yourself hours of time by not having to create a custom message for every single person.

Treat your social network profiles as if they are your OWN website. Be sure that your profile is ALL business. It should be clean, easy to read and all about your VO business. Try to keep personal stats to a minimum and make sure your phone and email info are highly visible.

Some social sites do not give you obvious spaces in which to place such info, so you may have to get creative. Many social sites allow you to post audio, so select an audio player for your demos that is easy to find and use. Uploading your audio to SoundCloud is a great way to get your material out there. This also gives you a unique web link, to include if the social site doesn't have any options for uploading audio.

Your biggest key to social network success is to make sure you are contacting and making friends with prospective clients. There's nothing wrong with making friends – but at some point you have to ask yourself if spending time talking with other talent on social networks is really helping to grow your business. Fraternizing with other talent may yield advice and tips about the industry, but it will not likely be a direct link to paying jobs.

Since social networks can be time-consuming, it may be wise to hire an outside marketing company or an assistant to manage the process. If, however you're willing to invest some time on nights and weekends, you'll be a social networking expert in no time. It will pay off. Social networking is the new standard in business marketing.

Social Networking Part 2:
There's So Much More Than Who Had Tuna for Lunch

If Facebook were a country, it would be the fourth most populated place in the world. This means it easily beats Brazil, Russia and Japan in terms of size and it just keeps growing.

LinkedIn has over 50-million members and 78% of recruiters use it to find applicants for jobs. LinkedIn also has very high Search Engine Optimization so profiles show high results in Google and Bing.

It took radio 38 years to reach 50 million listeners. Terrestrial TV took 13 years to reach 50 million users. The internet took just four years to reach 50 million people and in that same time, Facebook added 100 million users…so, why aren't you using social media?

Social Media is a great way to reach more people and increase the size of your network. You can connect with friends, voiceover colleagues and companies who hire talent. By being active in social media you have the ability to show your unique qualities and stay top-of-mind. You can also see what your competition is doing and stay ahead of them. Social Media helps you to be found, be in demand and be understood.

You can add yourself as a "fan" or "like" companies that you're interested in working with or learning more about. Many companies use Facebook to connect with potential applicants. Facebook pages are also indexed in search engines which increases the likelihood of folks finding your voice through a Google search. Twitter is an equally powerful tool.

If it all seems like too much to manage there are amazing, all-in- one, dashboard solutions that help you to manage all of your social media accounts at the same time. Some even offer SEO tools and more. HootSuite.com does all this and helps you to create a social media presence while developing your social persona. YouTube.com also offers hundreds if not thousands of videos on how to better use and understand social media. In fact at this point if it can be taught, you can find a tutorial on YouTube.

Chapter 5
Sales

Cold Calling and Sales – It's Time to Smile and Dial

Most of us in the voiceover industry are social creatures. We enjoy human contact and the personal relationships we build day to day. Knowing this, I find it curious how many voice talents HATE cold calling. Cold calling may not always be the best method to obtain new business, but when done well, it can get some great results.

From students who are brand new to industry veterans, folks always seem to cringe whenever they are prompted to "smile and dial". What's wrong? Seen the movie "Glen Garry, Glen Ross" one too many times? Or has text messaging and email made it so that we've forgotten how to be personal without a keyboard? Maybe the real problem is not the idea of making cold calls, but rather that most talent aren't sure how to properly cold call. That is a problem.

There's a lot of great business that talent can find just by picking up the phone. One of the best ways to tap into a new stream of revenue or get your name in an area of the industry that is new to you, is to hear the needs of an industry right from a client's mouth. Asking the right questions and staging your call is all it takes.

Always plan your call. Who are you looking for? What is the purpose of the call? What is the single most important thing you need to say? If you need to, make a few notes. Next, clear your mind, your desk, and your computer of all distractions.

The key to a great call is to sound confident but casual. Don't recite a sales pitch or turn your etiquette switch to Mary Poppins. Both are dead giveaways to the person on the other end that you are in fact selling something. Instead, take a friendly more familiar approach.

"Hey Bob, how've you been? It's good to talk to you. Everything good in your neck of the woods?"

Sure it may sound a little goofy at first, but isn't it similar to the way you'd speak to a client you've worked with for years? Keeping things casual can immediately disarm the person on the other end of the phone. Your familiarity will make them think you've spoken before and perhaps they forgot who you are. Either way, it sets the tone for the call and gives you a great "in". Then you can begin to introduce the reason for your call.

"So it's my understanding that you hire voice talent on a regular basis…"

If they say yes, you've now got an open door to offer your demo or to talk about your work. If they say no, don't apologize and end the call. Instead, ask a few leading questions.

"Then you must be using an ad agency. Who are you working with these days?" or *"Did I confuse you with someone else at your company?"*

You'll get info that will lead to your next call. Immediately call the person they mentioned. As soon as you get that party on the phone you'll want to say something like:

"Hi Sally I just spoke with Bob Smith and he gave me your name. Do you have a moment to chat…?"

Nothing you've said is misleading but you've effectively pulled off the always popular "name drop". A name drop ensures a person's attention because they have to assume you were sent to them for business purposes.

Another method I like is a more humble approach. For folks that are uncomfortable with the idea of making a "sales call", just make a fact-finding call. A company has to hear or accept your demo before they are even willing to talk about an actual project, so call a potential lead or contact and try saying:

"Hi Jim I came across your info and I'm looking for some help. I have a few questions and I think you're the person to ask. Is now a good time?"

You're being honest. The notion of asking someone for their help or assistance (and saying it genuinely) is very disarming. Make the person you are speaking with feel like they are accomplishing their good deed for the day and they'll provide the answers you need.

For more cold calling and sales techniques, pick up any of Zig Ziglar's books. They are packed with practical ways to make self- selling more comfortable. Also, it's wise to call companies who products or services you know, use, and enjoy. Big fan of a start-up with a great new face wash? Call them and express your loyalty and desire to work with them. It's a lot easier to initiate a call when you really do support and admire the company.

Lastly, try to admire great sales-people when you encounter them. Try adapting some of the techniques they used on you. You may come to find that you enjoy cold calling. Voice talent are great at it because we have skills and vocal control that most trained sales-people don't have. If you approach cold calls like you would an audition, it could change everything.

Pay to Play Websites – Navigating a Necessary Evil

In this next section we're going to talk about Pay to Play or Marketplace websites for voiceover actors. You may already be a P2P user, you might have a free profile, or you may be wondering what it's all about. We're going to discuss it all – in great detail.

I've been a pay to play user for years and while I don't profess to know everything about these websites, I do know what works and how to book jobs through them.

I want to advise against a common mistake with regard to pay to play services and websites. Many pay to play sites such as Voice123 and Voices.com offer talent a "webpage" on which to display their demos, bio, pictures, information, etc., so that clients who use those services can learn more about a talent they are considering for a booking.

These listing pages are definitely a bonus since they allow you the opportunity to have a certain measure of control over your paid profile. In addition, pay to play listings will often result in better search engine results since pay to play sites spend a lot of time and money optimizing their sites so that they rank high on search engines. Your pay to play list can be a huge benefit to your business model and marketing efforts when you piggyback on the company's efforts.

However, please do not mistake these portals or web pages for your OWN website. There is a big difference between having your own URL and having a Voice123 page. Many talent mistakenly present their pay to play listing pages as a self-owned website and if you are one of those talent you may not realize that this practice can hurt your business.
When you have a website all your own such as

www.SallySmithVO.com, you can send potential clients to a dedicated domain that is all about you, your skills and your talent. A self-owned URL gives you the freedom and control to create a space on the web where you can let the world know who you are by creating a brand identity that is unique to you. It makes the cost of investing in a website well worth it.

When you have a page on someone else's website (like in the case of a pay to play website) you are not sending a potential buyer to your little piece of the web. You are sending them to someone else's piece of the web. By doing so you run the risk that the client will find and use another voice – one of hundreds or even thousands of options available simply by searching the rest of the site.

The simple act of linking or directing a potential buyer to your pay to play listing is kind of like handing the ball to an opposing sports team right in the middle of a game. They may or may not score but you have now given them an advantage.

Pay to play sites can be excellent resources that allow you to promote your voice to the clients those sites serve, but your own website allows you to promote and market yourself on your terms by keeping a buyer focused on you and only you.

Searching the web can sometimes be an adventure in Attention Deficit Disorders. Think about how many times you have gone to a website to look for something and became distracted by something else entirely. It happens to most web users almost every day. Voiceover buyers are no exception. If you give them a chance to become side tracked or distracted they will wander. In this case, they may wander right out of your pay to play listing and into the loving arms of another talent.

Pay To Play Basics

I've been a P2P user for years as a talent. I've even competed with P2P sites as a casting director. For years I've heard both the horror and success stories of other voice actors as they navigate this, now common, way to find VO jobs.

This section is not here to bash pay to play or speak negatively of them, even though you'll hear many people do so. I know there is a lot of negativity about these sites. Talent have become increasingly frustrated with their lack of success or total loss of investment with pay to play sites. However, these services are not as mystifying as you think. Your own, realistic expectations are the key to having a successful pay to play experience.

The Biggest players in the pay to play voiceover world are currently Voice123, Voices.com, Bodalgo, Piehole, Voicebunny, VOPlanet, Internet Jocks, etc. but there are dozens more that pop-up all the time.

The most successful of these companies, (Voice123 and Voices.com) have been created by web geeks, not by voiceover people. The sites were not built for voiceover talent as they would make it appear, but rather as match-making (and ultimately money making) online networks.

Think of P2P sites like dating websites. They are made up of a database and an algorithm that mathematically computes and matches users. The program has a set of rules to follow (or points of compatibility). The database finds matches based on these rules. P2P sites are also search engines unto themselves - similar to Google and Yahoo. That's one of the ways that allows the thousands of site users (voiceover actors) to be found and sorted quickly by what they call voice seekers. The rest of the voiceover world calls these "voice seekers" clients.

Link building is an organic way to increase search engine results for a website. Site owners want to share links with other site owners to "organically" market their website. That's why P2P sites so badly want you to link your profile to your own website. It creates more links back to their site. I don't recommend doing this. Link your profile to your website but not your website to your P2P profile.

Pay to play sites spend lots and lots of money on web marketing and they target beginners. Most sites make big promises about how much money you can earn even if you have no experience. Don't fall into the hype. If you aren't a trained voiceover actor and you don't have a studio, proper demos, and a great marketing plan already in action, then P2P is not yet for you.

It takes being competent and competitive to make money on pay to play sites. Ignore anything these sites publicize about rates of pay, recording specs, studio info and any other advice. Most of it is skewed towards seekers and does little to benefit a budding voiceover actor.

The Algorithm

Remember learning basic mathematical logic in school? Logic is a form of probability. It operates under the following basis; "If this…then that." A pay to play algorithm has a very specific job, to find percentage matches based on data supplied from both voice seeker and voiceover talent. It seeks to find 100% matches first, and then categorizes remaining percentages (99%, 98%, 97%,) all the way down to zero. In most cases a system defaults to a predetermined setting (usually alphabetical order) after a certain match point. Meaning, search results under a 50% match will likely default to alphabetical order.

All this "matching" has one main purpose; to help a voice seeker (client) find the right voiceover actor for their project. When a client uses a site's automated system, the system's job is to find matches based on percentages. The first talent the system will reveal to the client or send an audition request to, is the ones closest to a 100% match; those folks get pushed to the top – and receive the job opportunity first.

Voice123's system is called Smart Cast. Voices.com denied that a "system" or algorithm existed for years – recently they named it Voice Match. I was the first voiceover coach to help talent understand this algorithm principle. Initially, all the P2P sites denied this was taking place. Now many of them publically post information about how their algorithm works.

The system being used to make matches can make or break your day. There are many ways in which you can make yourself a better match. We'll talk about that a little later in the profile section. First, I want to clarify a common pay to play scenario. A voiceover actor will say, "I'm at my PC and receive an audition request from Voices.com. As soon as I open it, 80 people have already responded! How is that possible?" It's because of the database. Top matches received first crack at the booking. You were a lower percentage match and therefore received the audition after the higher percentage folks and the premium or platinum tier members (folks who simply pay more money for better match placement.) Booking stats and feedback systems can also play a role in how soon you receive an audition vs. another talent. The better your stats, the sooner you'll see audition opportunities.

The average P2P site has between 3,000 and 6,000 users. Half to three-quarters of these users are men. So let's say 2,000 users are male. At least 50% of those men will fall into the 30-50 year-old, vocal age range. How many of these voice actors have used the words "announcer" "friendly" and "authoritative" to describe their voice? The results are overwhelming for a user.

Go to Google and search the word plumber. In less than 1 second I received 95,800,000 results. Now refine your search to include your city, state, and zip code… 82,400 results – more manageable (still overwhelming if you have a clogged toilet). Adding just a few pieces of critical info helped to eliminate more than 99% of the original search results. The same thing happens to voice seekers on P2P sites. They refine their searches in order to make very specific casting criteria. This way they have a few, quality results and not an overwhelming number.

Your Pay to Play Profile

The better job a website owner does of creating original unique content, the higher your search results will be in the average search engine. The same goes with pay to play sites. The only difference is it's an internal process (search results from a single website) not external (World Wide Web results from all websites).

So, how match friendly/unique is your listing profile? Come up with niche terms to describe what you do. This has a carryover effect on Google and other search engines too. The more complete and keyword populated your profile is the better you'll do. If your match criteria are better than someone else's you'll have better Pay to Play results.

Fill your profile and bio full of keywords - because you're not writing for people. Very few people are reading anything you write on a P2P site profile. Seekers don't really care about a lot of details. They don't want to know where you went to college, how many dogs you have or all the places you have lived. That's just fluff that takes up valuable key word space.

If you have a profile already, clear anything that is too general or any word that too many people are using. Words like warm, friendly, authoritative, guy/girl next door, are redundant terms at this point. Start thinking differently about how to describe your voice because that's what our clients are being forced to do.

I see a lot of talent create a story – the database does not understand this. It's developed to read keywords, adjectives, and descriptors. Create a list. Use unique keywords and strategically answer the call of specific clients. A good question to ask is; "what I am good at and what am I repeatedly getting jobs for?"

Also, content is king. The more you are tweaking your content and updating, the more success you will have. Why? Because words and phrases need to match what voice seekers are searching for and voiceover trends change.

The voice seeker experience usually starts with a client who doesn't really know what they want. Many are casting a voice for the first time. Many are uneducated about voiceover - and many are just cheap. When their search results are overwhelming, they refine the search.

The audio or demos you post to your profile needs to match the jobs you say you do. Or at the very least it must exist in order to support your claim. A common denominator with

P2P sites is that; the demos you showcase have to have text that describes the content of the demo to the listener. If your demo does not match its name and title then you have a big problem. If I say I do narrations, but don't specifically have a narration demo in my profile, the system will dock me and see it as a negative. It's not about convincing the client/seeker it's about convincing the database that you can back-up your claim!

Be a Client / Seeker

A great way to increase P2P success is to create a client account. Learn HOW to use the site before investing in a listing. Don't make a fake audition but pretend to be a buyer. Use the parameter from a recent audition you received and look at what a seeker sees. Search for yourself and use the terms and keywords that ID your voice and find your matching competition. You'll be shocked to see how many talent are using the same words to ID themselves. When you do this you will instantly be able to see other people you are up against. By taking these actions you'll be able to see yourself apart from and in relation to the competition.

How to Audition with P2P Sites

I call this training the puppy. The algorithm on most of these sites is intuitive. Meaning you can train it to respond to your likes and dislikes. Every time you answer an audition the system "notes" the dollar amount you answered and the job specifications. It will respond in kind by offering you future job choices that are similar. So if you answer jobs that are $500 - $1000 on average, the system will send you more of those types of jobs. Answer mostly $100 jobs and guess what you'll get more of?

When you answer or engage in low dollar jobs and set a minimum monetary amount for the jobs you will answer, it will be reflected with opportunities you see in the future. This will result in fewer auditions. Because the choice stuff is less frequent.

Set a minimum monetary amount for all auditions; be consistent and do not break that rule. I always prefer quality over quantity. I answer roughly 3 P2P auditions per day. These jobs book roughly every 2 to 3 weeks. Less is more. You don't need to answer 100s and 100s of auditions. Choice selection is critical. This is not a popular method us use in a system that most people want to 'milk' because they are paying for it. But it is a time saving method that allows you to expand your voiceover reach beyond just Pay to Play sites.

==Be proactive in deleting bad jobs, bad matches and bad dollar amounts, or things you don't have time for.== DELETE! Don't just let auditions sit there until they expire. Take time to work with the system and it will be more rewarding. This is especially true with Voice123.com.

When you're sending auditions send multiple takes. Include links and direct contact information. Don't answer any audition that more than 30 people have answered. The winner is usually in the first 10. When being asked to fill in a quote, you can, on some systems, type words not numbers. So you can say things like "flexible/negotiable based on terms". ==Auditions labeled as Budget TBD (To be determined) stink - don't answer them or do so sparingly.==

Flatter the client. It's always good to show a proactive approach and show that you are a team player. Show them you want to be a part of a successful campaign. It's all about finding a connection. Repeat clients are where success lies in P2P. And get them off of the P2P site and communicating with you directly ASAP.

Impact statements, jobs, and successes should be what you lead with in the comments section. Any legitimate credentials associated with a major brand should be emphasized. Voice seekers are 50% small to medium ad agencies and 50% individual or corporate agents seeking a voice for a one-time project.

When submitting audio files, edit your breaths and clicks before sending a finished file. Remember the clients are likely not casting directors or industry pros. They may not understand what an unedited read is. Don't watermark either. They will assume it's the result of a quality issue with your studio.
And lastly, be early. Your chance of booking decreases for every ten auditions that have been submitted ahead of you.

Both myself and J Michael Collins offer extensive P2P training to help voiceover actors become more proficient in how to use these sites and to help them increase their return on investment. P2P sites can be very, very effective tools but they can't be your only tool. If you find that almost all of your auditions come from pay to play sites, this is not a healthy or diversified business model. You must expand your efforts to both casting directors and agents in order to build a better-rounded voiceover business that is not solely dependent on one type of opportunity.

Chapter 6
Staying Focused

Business: A Judgment Free Work Zone

The English philosopher Herbert Spencer said, "There is a principle which is a bar against all information, which is proof against all arguments and which cannot fail to keep a man in everlasting ignorance - that principle is contempt prior to investigation." That's a mouthful, even for a voice talent. Simply translated, an open mind equals more business.

It's important to learn about new markets in which to offer your voiceover services. On a daily basis, I encounter many voiceover talent that are closing their minds to potential sources of new business because of misconceptions, fear, stereotypes and a lack of education. This is a big mistake and it might be time to see if you are keeping a closed VO mind instead of an open one.

Career consultants and coaches would be remiss if they did not encourage clients to pursue a broader range of money making opportunities, especially if they believe that a voice talent displays a good probability for success in a new venture. Unfortunately, I find that recommendations are often pooh-poohed by talent who possesses a self-defeating attitude.

There are two excuses I hear regularly: "That's just not what I do" and "I don't know enough about that industry to make it successful for me." Either statement is not something wise business-people would say.

Diversification is a critical element in financial success. There are many voiceovers you can specialize in, but to ignore or avoid any area of the voice industry (that can earn you more money) is just foolish.

You may find yourself voicing for audio books when your true passion is movie trailers. You may also find that your bills are paid and your efforts in audio books are strengthening your performance capabilities and allowing you to have more money to invest in trailer training and marketing.

Pigeon-holing yourself into only one type of voiceover in a soft economy is also a bad idea because your business is only as good as your last booking. If your chosen area of VO starts to suffer a decline, your business will suffer a decline as well.

This means you are not taking the reins and running your own company; this leaves you at the mercy of the industry. Ask yourself, do you want to be a follower or a proactive entrepreneur?

Before you were a voice talent, you weren't one. Why should you stop the learning process now? Find out more about the other industries you are not marketing your voice to. If your excuse for not diversifying is a lack of education, well, that's just dumb.

VO talent have many outstanding options for training and coaching that will help you to learn the ways to start in and later dominate a type of voiceover that is new to you.

You can also find out more about an industry just by reading their trade magazines. Virtually every industry has a trade organization, website or publication of some kind. There are even trade magazines for message-on-hold and IVR work. This is one of the best ways to find contact information for new clients and find out about their needs.

Are your old ideas keeping you from creating a successful

VO business? Take the time to learn about areas you don't know and areas you think you know. VO changes rapidly, so you might be holding on to some outdated concepts that are no longer valid. Keep an open mind and your business will flourish.

VO JOBS YOU ARE SKILLED IN AND ABLE TO PERFORM	VO JOBS YOU SHOULD EXPLORE AND CONSIDER

Desperation Stay Away

Like love, desperation is difficult to define because it's intangible, yet, you know it when you see it. It has a feel that can leave you with mixed emotions. Pity, disgust, contempt and occasionally nervous laughter can all be elicited from a desperate attempt to reach a voiceover buyer. Do you reek of desperation?

In every communication you have, desperation can be heard and felt. Some even say it has a smell. To avoid the stink, you should scrutinize every email, demo package and letter you use to solicit your voice. Ask the same two questions:

"Do I sound like someone pleading for work?"

"Am I trying too hard to convince someone of how great and worthy I am of their time and attention?"

Your goal is to come across as a confident, busy, working voiceover actor; however, if your cold calls and written text make you sound like a telemarketer or someone who is obviously trying to sell the recipient, you are probably getting a less-than-desirable result from your efforts.

Today's business-people are just as hardwired as the general public to avoid and dislike "sales" calls. An obvious attempt to sell your services will turn your potential client off to further communications with you as your efforts represent (in their mind) the departure of their dollars.

Instead, try to sound like a professional business partner. A cool, casual, less-rehearsed style will signal to the other party that they are communicating with another business professional and that a mutually beneficial relationship is at stake. Don't let a potential client feel that you need them as this will signal their desperation receptors. A relaxed approach will help them to understand that you need each other.

In written form, keep things short and sweet. You are a voiceover talent, dammit! OF COURSE you are "available for auditions, ready to work, able to send custom demos, have a professional studio and are versatile." That is the very definition of what voice talent do. Don't bludgeon your customers with information they have heard a thousand times. Overstating your "professionalism", "attention to detail" and your "willingness to work" will send your desperate plea wafting in the direction of the client.

So what's the alternative? Keep it simple. If you are less than two years into your voice business and you are still "in-training", it may seem to you that you have nothing to offer a potential client. That's your fear talking and fear is desperation's best buddy. You cannot be afraid to approach potential business nor should you postpone or prolong the process because you feel that you are not prepared to do so.

The average client has no reason to doubt that you are anything less than you claim to be. If you say you're a pro and carry yourself like one, a potential client will accept this. Don't attempt to procure a major LA or NY agent with this approach. They will see through your veiled attempt. However, local chamber of commerce members and locally owned businesses have no reason NOT to believe you.

Small and local clients can help to validate your new career simply because they see you as someone with more knowledge of VO than them, and that is very likely true. You probably know far more about voiceover than your dentist. So if you tell him you are a professional talent, able to record a more professional-sounding voiceover for his message-on-hold system, he will not doubt you.

You must believe that your skills are worthy, that your voice is worthy and most importantly you must believe with all your heart that the skills you possess are valuable. You are not just another person looking for a job; you are a business owner who offers a valuable service to other businesses.

If you doubt yourself at all, that little thing called desperation will seep into your pores and out of your mouth or onto a page. Take this to heart – go clean out your office, dust off your studio equipment and while you're at it, dust off the desperation too. It will be the best thing you do for your business this year.

The Economy of Voiceovers

When the economy is soft, advertising budgets are often the first to be cut or altogether removed by many companies. A great majority of voiceover work comes from advertising. Talent that rely heavily on commercial work should explore other areas of the industry to account for the losses they may suffer in a soft economy. Even when times are tough, never make rash decisions and offer cut-rate quotes in an attempt to increase your bookings. The idea of quoting low may become appealing, but please try not to offer a temporary bargaining chip that can have longer term and more devastating results on our industry as a whole. Think about the future.

Let's say, for example, that you quote well below the norm for a job today. You book the job partially because the price was too appealing for the client to pass up. A month from now, that client comes back for more and expects the same price. Times are still hard, so you agree. Before you know it this is a steady client that you hear from often.

That's great for the short-term, but as the economy gets better, it's not as if you're going to suddenly be able to convince this client that they should pay you more. You have set a precedent. This precedent rings loud and clear for budget-minded clients and it says, "I don't need to pay more than X for a voiceover because it's not worth it." You have potentially set a client loose into the VO populace that is going to insist on substandard rates

When the economy is poor, know that it will get better. It's only temporary. So, it's wise to take these times to focus on new strategies and alternative types of work. It's also wise to hold steady to your standard rates.

Consider offering incentives or one-time discounts as a way to attract new clients, but always make it clear that clients are receiving a deal or a sale which implies that the price is only being discounted for a short time.

Voice actor John Taylor told me a great story about a client that was offering subpar rates of pay. This client could not understand why John was charging the rate he was (not by any means an astronomical figure by the way; it was fair pay for the job). John explained firmly but politely to the client that they were not just paying for a VO. Make sure your clients understand that they are paying for your time, your professionalism, your experience, your training, your dedication, your skill and yes, your voice, too.

If talent work together to unify these ideas, it will go a long way towards setting a higher standard for our industry and help all of us weather tough economic times.

The True Cost of Success

VO students often want to know one thing – "How long is it going to take me to be able to replace my income with enough VO work so that I can leave my job and do voice work full time?" Well, that depends. How quickly do you want to leave your job?

The average person in the United States earns anywhere from $35,000 to $50,000 per year. We all know the value of a dollar and the idea of replacing $50,000 of annual income can seem overwhelming. Voice talent benefit from looking at a simple economic model that makes covering their expenses and income replacement seem a lot more manageable.

Let's say that you need to earn $50,000 a year in order to leave your existing job. $50,000, divided by 12 months, is $4,167. This number is your monthly VO goal. Not quite as scary. Now divide that monthly goal by 4 and you get $1,041. This is your weekly VO goal. Wow, it's getting even less scary. Now take it one step further. Divide that number by 5 work days of the week and you get $209. Can you make $209 a day in VO?

When you break your earning goals down in this manner, you take some of the stress out of that huge annual number and you are able to see a more realistic mark. In reality, $200 a day is very manageable when you consider that, most non-union VO jobs pay more than that on average. This means that your goal is to book enough VO jobs in a day to equal or exceed this amount. Depending on the area of VO you are specializing in and the types of clients you are looking to obtain, you are then able to calculate your earnings potential based on the types of clients that will hire you.

If your goal is to be a TV promo or radio imaging talent, then in order to earn $50,000 a year, you will need to book 14 stations on retainer that pay you $300 per month. This means you will need to book 1 station every 3.7 weeks in order to replace your annual income. Suddenly your goal becomes a very realistic endeavor. Hopefully, most of the stations will then be ongoing year to year, so you have those contracts, PLUS new ones in the second year, then more in the 3rd and so on. If you are a non-union commercial talent and you are targeting small market clients, an average commercial job will likely pay you (at the very least) $100.00. This means you'll need to book roughly 500 commercial jobs in a year or 2 $100 spots per day.

Now the harder part. Waking up every day, going to your computer and asking yourself: "How am I going to earn $200 dollars in VO work today?

This simple method is used by small business owners, service providers and retailers around the country every day. When you know you're goal, it's easier to offer sales, incentives and to implement marketing strategies that make it easier to make you daily goal a reality. You are also able to see a realistic day-to-day tracking of your productivity and earnings. This is a critical foundation of success for every business.

No one can tell you exactly how successful you'll be in voiceovers. You'll have good days and bad. But if you employ this 'one day at a time' method, you'll likely be able to leave your current full-time job faster than you thought possible.

My Earning Goals

I need to earn $_____per year.

Which equates to $_____ per month.

Which equates to $_____ per week.

Which equates to $_____ per work day.

Setting S.M.A.R.T Goals

For years, I spent each day, as both a Voiceover Career Consultant and Casting Director (at VoiceHunter.com) reading and reviewing dozens of VO evaluations. These requested forms gave me great insight into the problems and challenges facing VO talent. The last question we asked on the form was, "What current career goals may we help you with?" I found time and again that most talent had and still have, no idea how to determine or define their business goals.

"More work", "better bookings", "more notable credits", are not goals, but desires and it's important to know the difference. We all desire more work and higher pay, but few voiceover talent know how to get there. The key to success is to set goals that are Specific, Measurable, Attainable, Realistic and Timely. Goals help you to take control, stay focused and achieve greatness. If you want to be the best talent, you can be, then remember to stay S.M.A.R.T.

"I'd like to book national commercials."
All of your goals should be specific. With a goal like this, you are able to better illustrate the type of work you are looking to book and the level at which you'd like to achieve it. From this statement, you are able to begin evaluating and researching the steps needed to achieve your goal. Of course, different goals will require different actions, but in this case, by being specific, you can create a clear focus.

"I'd like to book 10 national commercials."
Your goals should be measurable. This change to your goal statement defines a clear number of commercials that you'd like to book; in this case, 10. Your focus now has an even more specific direction.

What will it take to book 10 more national commercials? It could be a variety of things: more training, obtaining another agent, revising your demo, etc. The answers will be specific to your situation and will allow you to start creating a plan of action that lays out, step by step, the route you'll take to reach your goal. You can also track and measure your distance to the finish line as you begin to cross things off your action list and track your progress.

"I'd like to book 10 national commercials this week."
Next, test your goals for attainability. In order for '10 national commercials this week' to be attainable, you must have the skills, abilities and financial wherewithal necessary to reach your goal. Is it possible to book 10 more national commercials? If you are an experienced talent who has booked national work in the past, it might be. Is it possible to attain 10 national commercial bookings this week? Even the best of the best might struggle with that goal.

If you're a new talent, what is attainable might be your first national, while skilled pros can set higher goals for themselves. Don't set the bar too high, though. You'll find yourself in a position of fast frustration if your goal is not attainable due to the reasons mentioned here. Take an honest, personal inventory of your skill, experience and finances to determine the attainability of your goal.

"I'd like to book 10 national commercials this month."
A goal must represent an objective toward which you are both willing and able to work. Assuming that you are willing, what you really have to determine is… are you able? Be careful what you wish for. You need to be capable of realistically handling the work-load and the expectations attaining the goal will

generate. You may want 10 more national commercials this month but can you effectively handle 10 more national commercials and deliver quality work to the clients you already have? If a goal has the potential to jeopardize or harm your existing business, then it is an unrealistic goal.

"I'd like to book 10 national commercials this year."
Finally we come to the matter of timeliness. You will need a time frame for your goal and this can be tricky to determine. The bigger the goal, the more time you should give yourself to attain it. Setting a one year goal to book 10 more national commercials is a good time frame.

Even if the goal ends up taking a year and 3 months, you won't be disappointed in the end. Give yourself too little time and you'll create an anxious and overly stressful situation that might lead to failure. Likewise, too much time can be a problem. If you have a tendency to procrastinate, don't set lengthy time frames. Give a teenager three days to take out the trash and he'll wait till the last moment! Don't fall into the same trap. Organize goals by size, and don't delay in getting them done.

Recommended Products

Below is information on how to purchase all the products and services recommended in this workbook.

Quick Books
(www.Intuit.com) or call (877)-683-3280. The Intuit family of accounting products also offers low-cost, DIY website solutions.

FreshBooks
(www.freshbooks.com) – online, cloud based accounting and book keeping.

Neat Receipts
(www.neat.com) - IRS compliant expense scanner.

Microsoft Office Small Business Edition (includes Word, Excel, etc.)
www.microsoft.com or purchase at a local retailer such as Best Buy.

Google Drive / Sheets / Forms (comes with a Gmail account)
Much like the Office Suite above, Google has similar tools that stay in your Google Drive cloud so they're always accessible - even on your phone! There are tons of uses, especially for collaboration with multiple people seeing real-time updates as you make them.

Performer Track
(www.performertrack.com)– an excellent talent industries contact management and day-planner tool.

Fax Zero
(www.faxzero.com) – virtual fax service that lets you send and receive faxes via email.

DocuHub
(www.dochub.com) - Allows you to edit, sign and send any PDF online for free! You can even save directly into your Google Drive or Dropbox.

Windows Defender
(Windows OS feature) – anti-virus/spyware/ malware system for your computer. A google search can give you more info on how to enable the program. I DO NOT recommend using any other virus protection software.

Malwarebytes
(www.malwarebytes.com) – free version removes ANY virus, infection or malware that makes it on to your computer.

Disk Cleaner
(Windows OS feature)- use this to clean up any temporary files that could be cluttering your system. Act! (www.act.com) – a sales tool used around the world by sales forces at companies large and small.

Plaxo
(www.plaxo.com) – contact management system.

Paypal
(www.paypal.com) – receive and send money in fast, secure, online transactions.

VO Edit By Design
(www.VoEditByDesign.com) – A production and editing

company just for VO talent.

Meet-Up.com
(www.Meetup.com) – A social network site dedicated to face to face meetings between groups of users.

Radio Mall
(www.radiomall.com) – a supplier of contact leads for the radio and TV industries.

Salesgenie
(www.salesgenie.com) – A supplier of contact leads in almost every industry.

SnapPages
(www.snappages.com) – Do It yourself website creation.

Wix
(www.wix.com) – Do it yourself website creation for a slightly higher cost.

GoDaddy
(www.godaddy.com) - Domain and hosting available for purchase along with website solutions and services.

Gabrielle Nistico
(www.gabriellenistico.com) – coaching, career assistance, demos, websites, books and more.

Helpful Apps

As our society is becoming increasingly reliant on our smart phones, more and more companies are developing apps that make our lives as self-employed voice actors much easier. Note that some apps maybe only be available for Apple OS, and not Android (or vice versa).

MileIQ

This app will keep track of all the miles you drive on a daily basis. You then categorize which drives are for business and which were personal. The app saves this info away for tax season! The best part? It's IRS approved! It also doesn't kill your battery!

Google Drive

A great way to keep your files always accessible. The app is particularly useful when you need review / edit / send a file immediately – even on the go.

Hiya

A great, free, caller ID and call blocker app. Helps to filter and screen telemarketers. This app uses whitepages.com to determine who's for real and flags potential spams based on previous reports. A window will pop up on top of your phone call, so you know not to answer!

TinyScanner

A scanner app that turns android and apple devices into a portable document scanner that can scan everything as images or PDFs. With this app you can scan documents, photos, receipts, reports, just about anything.

Expensify

Organize all your receipts in one place! Take a photo of your receipt and their SmartScan automatically finds the relevant info and inputs it into the app. It has great travel features too! It also integrates with Quickbooks and a list of other accounting software.

OfferUp
A great place to find used deals on equipment gear and acoustic treatment.

Twisted Wave
An easy way to edit audio files when you're on the road.

Notes:
Use the space below to create any additional notes related to your VO business studies.

_____
_____
_____
_____
_____
_____
_____
_____
_____
_____
_____
_____
_____
_____

Chapter 7
Voiceover Agents

Intro to Agents

Because you are reading this guide, I must assume a few things about you, the reader.

You are either:
- Looking for a voiceover agent.
- You have an agent, but want additional representation.
- You have an agent and the relationship has yielded little, so you want to pursue new representation.

I'm going to do my best in this guide to address your specific situation and help you obtain your agent goals. We're going to start with some basics about the agent and talent relationship. Everyone wants an agent. But sometimes I think talent want an agent for the wrong reasons. In all the years that I have worked with talents and talent agents, I have found that the talents who have excellent working relationships with their agents are those that set realistic goals with regard to their representation. It's all about expectation management.

The Agent Myth

One of the greatest myths in the voiceover industry is that ALL it takes to be successful and "make it big" is to get on a major voiceover agent's roster. There is a lot to be said for working with a well-known and reputable agent; but, an agent is not where the proverbial VO buck stops.

Agents are NOT the Holy Grail of work. Many talent make the mistake of thinking a good agent is all it takes to be successful and that once they have a reputable agent, the burden of success is in the agent's hands. That is not so! Your agent is a part of your team, but you still need to be proactive in your business.

I work with a lot of respected VO agents and a lot of respected talent. Both agree that the most successful talent are those who actively employ agent driven marketing as well as their own. I have also seen a lot of talent who, unfortunately, rest on their laurel's and say; "I've made it now that I'm repped! I never have to look for work again." Not so, my friends, not so. This guide is designed to help you understand how to get signed to voiceover agent rosters, however I want to help you temper your expectations and have realistic goals as it relates to agents.

Talent that fall into the trap of believing their agents are the end- all-be-all of bookings live in a fantasy that ends with ill-will towards their excellent and well respected former-agent. Former, of course, being the operative word. As with any relationship proper expectation management is critical.

If you find yourself in this position - dumping your agent may be something to reconsider. Instead, look to supplement the efforts of your agent with a new strategy. Talk to your agent about the things you can do to help market and promote yourself in addition to their efforts.

The Truth About Agents

Agents do create and distribute marketing materials using a variety of the latest technologies to reach industry professionals who might hire you. However, these marketing efforts are not usually specific to any one talent on the agent's roster. These efforts exist to bolster the agency as a whole. Simply put, a talent agent doesn't care all that much who, specifically, books a gig - as long as someone on their roster does.

This is why engaging in your own, individual and supplemental marketing is critical. Every VO talent should take measures on their own to bring attention to their unique skills and abilities with or without an agent! Working in conjunction with and communicating with your agent is however crucial, to ensure the best end results. Even top-dog, big-city voiceover agents like TGMD, William Morris, Abrams Artists, SBV and DPN all greatly support the efforts their talent make towards marketing themselves.

In most cases your agent will even offer their advice when it comes to creating the best possible presentation, and why wouldn't they? Any marketing you do benefits you both.

Some agents will give you step-by step instructions as to demo changes, website tweaks and other critical adjustments needed in your presentation - more on this later.

A few years back I asked Dean Panaro of Abrams Artists in LA, (formerly of DPN) why he appreciates it when a talent on his roster actively markets their skills and he said:

"Because of technology VO has truly become a national business. Actors in Miami and San Francisco are reading for the same projects as actors in NY and LA.
The talent pool has become super saturated. Literally, producers have too many choices. Actors that execute smart and specific targeted marketing plans can give themselves a distinct advantage."

When asked the same question, regarding her famous voice-actor client Joe Cipriano, Mary Ellen Lord from SBV Talent replied, "In business it is all about the connection. If a talent makes a personal connection with a buyer, it makes it that much easier to suggest and sell them on a project. Joe is a personable, memorable guy."

The Agent Plan

I presume that since you now own this guide, you are planning to take measures to market yourself to voiceover agents and these pages will hopefully assist you in the those efforts. But, if you don't have a marketing plan in effect for yourself - outside of agents - there's no time like the present. It all starts with a killer brand that well defines the sound of your voice and the industry you service. Working with a voiceover coach, brand and marketing coach like myself (details at GabrielleNistico.com) will help with this big first step.

Then use a combination of direct mail campaigns, websites and web advertising, newsletter blasts and blogs - all proven and effective ways to self-promote your voice. Set aside a small percentage of your earnings into a marketing budget to help you accumulate the funds needed.

Don't try to blanket an industry, instead chose proven, targeted methods. For instance, if TV promo is your goal, construct a specific plan, message, (even website) for those specific buyers. The TV Promo buyer is unlike any other, with needs, wants, expectations and challenges all their own.

Speak directly to a buyer on all fronts and you prove yourself an expert in that area of voiceover.

If your material is well presented and you give your marketing campaign time to work – it will work! Consult with your agent, a voiceover marketing expert and other talent about where your money is best invested.

This proactive approach eliminates all sorts of unnecessary pressure. It shows you that you can be a self-reliant business owner, capable of bringing in business on your own. And, these self-marketing efforts prior to, or side-by-side with an agent campaign can do a few very valuable things for you:

A: The better your brand, the clearer it is, the easier a time an agent will have determining how they can sell you and subsequently where and how you fit into their current roster. ==A great brand can significantly elevate your worth to an agent.==

B: It proves to a potential agent that you are a ==go-getter== who is ==self-motivated== and that you are a success motivated, business-minded actor. Translation: not a prima-donna who fancies themselves an artist, but rather a working actor who wants to stay busy and keep working.

And most importantly, it shows that you are someone who isn't going to rely solely on your agent to get you work. Sometimes, being clear about that will get you the golden ticket onto an agent's roster.

More Agent Myth-Busting
The Mythical Creatures of Old and Today's Agent

Before I explore the specifics of how to submit to an agent, I want to cover all the bases and make certain you understand how an agent works, the things they do, the things they don't do and the things they can't do. The voiceover talent that are most likely to be signed are always those that are educated about an agent's business and practices.

An agent is one person or can be an entire company of people that represent you as a performer. An agent works to book you jobs, get you auditions and negotiates terms and payments on your behalf.

You might have this image in your mind of a Hollywood agent of old - or an Ari Gold-like character from the more recent, HBO show, Entourage. (The character was loosely based on Ari Emanuel - a real life agent icon at William Morris Endeavor) Either way the stereotype that is perpetuated is that agent and actor have these meaningful, in-depth relationships and that the agent invests oodles of time cultivating and grooming them. It's a bit Cinderella-like in the way it's typically presented.

The stereotype also dictates that the agent spends exorbitant amounts of time obtaining specific projects and hard-ball negotiating 'the deal' for their actor. Notice that I've been saying 'actor'. Singular. That's because that is the biggest lie in this fairytale. Unless of course you are Julia Roberts.

A-List actors get super-star treatment and attention from their agents. Top actors from TV and film enjoy the special agent relationship outlined earlier. And yes they enjoy all the glitz that you'd expect from a Hollywood agent; sprawling, glittering glass offices, sparkling Perrier on tap, all in a high-rise overlooking The Hollywood Hills. Why? Because when each project the agent negotiates is worth 10s of millions - this is what you'd expect.

That's not exactly how voice acting works. Voice actors don't see that kind of fame. So here's what you can reasonably expect: Small agencies with a small staff. Yes - even some of the LARGEST voiceover agents in NY and LA - the real heavy hitters, are just a few folks (usually no more than 5) in a well-appointed but casual office.

In smaller markets agencies are 1 or two man shops, in average, modest digs. In either case you can expect that there are a lot of other actors on the voiceover roster - making their client list pretty full. As a result they have only a small amount of time for personal attention for each talent.

Voiceover agents survive on volume, not a few block-buster bookings per year. This means they work feverishly every day to compete against other agents, casting services and online marketplaces for enough projects each month to pay staff, cover expenses and turn a profit. It's really not so glamorous.

Yes, they are usually rather nice and very willing to talk to you and assist you - to a point. If they are super busy or in the middle of a booking - expect that they won't have time for you.

In the past voiceover agents promoted your work. Really promoted by sending your demo reel or CD in droves to casting directors and potential clients. They sold the individuals on their rosters and their rosters were small. They molded, they groomed, and they helped shape parts of your career.

Today's voiceover agent is very good at selling your skills to an individual buyer, negotiating the best rate with the client and making sure you get paid in a timely fashion.
You should see your agent (or a potential agent) as someone who can negotiate excellent rates and terms on your behalf and someone who will increase your exposure and get you auditions. Your agent should also assist you with advice on your demos, auditions and over-all presentation.

And lastly, your agent should be someone who can add to your credibility as a professional talent. You status on a roster should be something you feel good and proud to boast about.

Your modern agent will not tell you exactly what to do but will instead make suggestions. It's up to you to seek-out and implement their occasional guidance. If your agent tells you to do something, it's wise to do it. They know their buyers and the expectations of those buyers. So, if your agent wants a new demo, new website or new audition style from you, implement those changes as soon as possible. They aren't going to ask / tell you twice.

Who Should I Approach?
Union Agents, Non Union, or Both

The answer depends on your current and future union plans as well as the areas of VO in which you specialize. Either way it's critical to know and understand the type of agent you are approaching before you approach.

A union agent only negotiates / deals in union (SAG-AFTRA) bookings and only represents unionized performers.

A non-union agent deals in mostly non-union jobs and the occasional union job.

A union agent will typically want an exclusive contract with you, the performer, which locks you in to only working with them in a particular geographic territory. The agent's coverage zone could be the whole of the US (if they are bi-costal and have more than one office), it could be a large region (the North East) or an entire coast.

The contract will typically state that any and all work that you receive in that geographic region must be brought to, negotiated by and is subject to a percentage fee by the agency. They effectively own a piece of all the work you do in that territory. The contract will also bar you from working with another agent in that same geography.

When getting paid for a union job, all you have to do is keep track of the work you've done and who owes you what. The union and your agent do the rest.

Union agencies are typically much harder to get into. They are in large markets, (NY, LA, Chicago) and the acting competition in these areas is fierce. Many of these agents don't believe they ever need to work with talent outside of these cities because - 'all the talent they could ever need is right here'. That can make it difficult, (but not impossible) to get them to consider you if you live out of the area.

A non-union agent may request the same sort of geographic contract as a union agent (however their territories are usually very small - a state or city). Some non-union agents only enforce a policy whereby they take a commission of work they bring you. So they effectively act less like an agent, and more like a casting company.

Most agents have more talent than they need and only seek someone new when there's a hot trend or they feel the roster is getting a little stale. Union agents only want to work with the best and most capable talent – those that will get lots of work. After all, that's how the agency makes their money.

Union agents typically operate under a 'no-unsolicited material/referral only' policy when it comes to new roster submissions. This means that the agency will not look at your email, open a package or engage you in anyway unless your material is coming directly to them from someone they already know and trust. This person must usually be a talent on their roster, a casting client or another agent. Non-union agents will usually take a chance on a lesser-known, newer talent.

Follow the referral rule - otherwise you are wasting time and money contacting these agents. It typically takes many years to get to the point of a referral. Why? Because someone else has to be willing to stick their neck out for you...you have to be AMAZING - not just good. Getting a referral takes creating carefully cultivated relationships with other actors.

Non-union agents are pretty approachable and open to receiving info from new talent at almost any time. They will review your CD, your email, your website etc. ...eventually. It may take them as much as 3 months to get around to listening to your material because they receive 100's if not thousands of submissions a month.

No news is bad news. An agent will not delay in calling or reaching out to a talent they are interested in working with. They want you on their roster before their competition gets you. So if they like you, they move fast.

Occasionally an agent will send a rejection letter. These letters are pretty generic. They will commend your skill, tell you that they simply don't have room on the roster for you right now and that you should submit again in the future. They mean the very last part. The rest is the easiest, nicest way they know to let you down.

Don't let it discourage you - keep making improvements and try again with that agent in 6 months or a year. Follow up calls and emails to union agents should be kept to a minimum. They are largely a wasted effort.

In all honesty if the agent isn't reaching out to you, they aren't interested. There really isn't much point in calling or emailing to see if they received your material and had a chance to review it. Instead, just add them to your marketing list and send them periodic updates about your work and accomplishments.

If you follow-up too much or too often it will make you come across as needy, demanding and possibly just plain annoying. Try with another agent instead. It's a much better use of your time. Likewise don't try to guilt or buy your way onto a roster.

Legalities
Know How to Pick a Legitimate Agent

Many talents have representation in every region in the country. The more folks you have working for you the better. Yes, you are allowed to have more than one agent - some voiceover talent have upwards of a dozen agents - some foreign, most domestic. How many agents you can have depends largely on your union status and the restrictions already in place from the contracts you have signed previously with other agents.

Knowing how to pick them is critical. Just because an agent wants you...doesn't mean you want them. Some are flat-out scams and sometimes a little extra investigation reveals that they are just up to something no good.

Here are all the things a legally operating agent CANNOT do:

- They cannot force you to spend money with them or with specific individuals on classes, coaches, demos, website or other services in exchange for or as a contingency of being signed to their roster.

  As an example, they cannot say - "You must get your demo made with Judy Smith and take 6 of her classes before I'll sign you." They CAN say - "You need a new demo. I'd recommend you work with Gabby Nistico, Julie Williams or Chuck Duran. Regardless when you have a new demo let's chat again and discuss possible roster placement."

- They cannot charge more than 10% commission on a union booking. They should not exceed more than 20% commission on a non-union booking.

Non-union booking are unregulated - therefore the agent can charge whatever they like for commissions. I've heard as high at 40% from some agencies. These are just poor unethical practices and should be considered unacceptable terms.

- An agent cannot force you to turn over pre-existing work. Many agents will seek out a talent because they want to start taking commission on work you had prior to them being your agent.

  They want the ability to renegotiate those deals, have access to residual earnings and handle all new bookings from that pre-existing work-source. This can be very lucrative for them. And it can be useless to you. You want a relationship that focuses on new business.

- An agent cannot charge you a fee (flat or annual) in exchange for representation. They only earn money from work they bring in or negotiate for you. There's no other way for them to capitalize on your association.

- Not technically a 'legality' but I always recommend that you take the time to research an agent's roster of talent. If the talent they rep are mostly newbies who are making rookie mistakes or you feel that the roster is way, way, oversaturated; chances are, something is fishy. An agent is only as good as their talent. You want to be in with the best, not the best of the worst.

Presentation
Perception Matters Most

I assume you have a killer demo. Not a decent demo, not a good demo, not a great demo, but a holy-crap-this-person-is-so- amazing-I-must-sign-them-NOW demo. If you don't, get it fixed pronto.

I also assume that you have an equally impressive website. Sharp and clean, full of bold statements, and bolder graphics. If not, you aren't agent ready.

An agent looks to your existing marketing material (demo and website mainly) as a way to gauge a few things about you.

1: How skilled and in-demand you are.

2: How effective have you been thus far at creating your own success.

It's all about perceptions. You have to spin your voiceover story to make it dazzling and appealing. Say the bare minimum in written form. Nothing will matter as much as the demo they hear.

Whether you are writing a cover letter, a website homepage or an email - say it with the least amount of words possible. They don't care about your life story, where you went to school, how long you have been training or about the 400 car dealer spots you did last year. They want to know:

What you sound like: Describe your voice and its uses - colorfully and with engaging, active-tense language.

What you specialize in: The thing that you're 'the best' at - the area of the industry in which you are kicking ass and taking names.

That you aren't a newbie: Even if you are - they don't need to know that. Give a confident, professional air and they won't even question how long you've been doing this.

The fastest way for them to snoop out a newbie?

Desperation. Newbies always sound desperate to work with an agent. Any agent. And they say the most painfully obvious things. In a stack of over 100 recent agent submissions almost every letter read the same way. The example below is an accurate representation of how painfully boring and uninspired these letters are.

Dear Agent,
"My name is Sally. I'm a professional voice actress. I've enclosed my demo for your consideration. I'm available for auditions any time and I'd be happy to show you what I can do for your clients. Please keep me in mind for commercial, narration, industrial, e-learning and audio book projects. I've been training with Coach Lenard Bumgarden for over 6 months. I can be reached at 555-123-4567."

Here's the agent translation of the same letter.

"My name is Sally and I'm a professional voice actress. **(No crap)** *I'm sending you my material in order to be considered for your talent roster.* **(Yeah I know, you're a talent, I'm an agent - why else would you be reaching out to me?)** *I've enclosed my demo for your consideration.* **(No sh*t Sherlock - I can feel it in the package/I see it in the email)** *I'm available for auditions any time* **(You'd better be)** *and I'd be happy to show*

you what I can do for your clients. **(Well, what would that be EXACTLY?)** *Please keep me in mind for commercial* **(If your demo doesn't suck),** *narration* **(Again, if your demo doesn't suck),** *industrial* **(I don't cast those),** *e-learning* **(or those),** *and audio book projects. I've been training with coach Lenard Bumgarden for over 6 months.* **(Hey - so you are a newbie and you have a crappy coach - suspicions confirmed!)** *I can be reached at 555-123-4567."*

Brutal - yes. Sadly, an all too common occurrence. Most talent simply fail to realize that they are the 15th person today to submit to this agent's roster and only a select few will stand-out. You have to make some different choices in order to be the one that stands out. Find original ways to make your point.

Stay away from anything too conservative or corporate. Agents are not in a conservative business. And you, as an actor are allowed to be a little eccentric and a little bold in your choices.

Read up on public relations tactics, cross reference your brand and your marketing message and then construct the message you want to send to a potential future agent.

The rule is the same one it's always been in show-business - keep them wanting more. Say too much, do too much, write too much and they get bored with you fast. Instead tease, entice, and make them want to know more about you.

Usually the best VO cover letters read like this:

"Hi, I've heard great things about your agency from some fellow actors who are on your roster; Bob, Joe and Robin. I'm interesting in seeing how we can create a mutually beneficial relationship too. Give me a call sometime if you like my work. I look forward to the possibility of a prosperous partnership."

Short, sweet and once a salutation is complete - speaks the agent's language $$$$$$$$$$! Make no mistake you as a voice actor represent one thing and one thing only to a potential agent -- dollar sign.

If they don't smell the money coming off of you, hear money in your reads, see money on your website - they won't contact you.

Here's a great cover letter example from Doug Turkel:

"You know how every time you show up at a party, there's always that one beefy guy with the "monster truck" voice who hears what you do and explains how EVERYONE tells him he should do voiceovers?

I'm not that guy.
I'm the guy people go to when they specifically don't want that guy.

Over the years, I've quietly become the voice behind 10,000 spots and a few TV networks. So while you may never have heard of me, you have certainly heard me. And I've done it all from my home base in Miami, without major market representation. Which is why I'm writing to you.

I'd love the opportunity to talk about our possibilities, I think we can do well together."

Part of your job is to know the difference between an on-screen actor resume and a voiceover resume. Voiceover only agents can be very put-off by on-camera submissions. Agents who do a little of everything; theater, print, modeling, on-camera and voiceover - need to be able to quickly distinguish what it is you do.

An on-screen actor's resume usually includes height, weight, specific role details, production companies, etc. Voiceover clients and agents don't require any of those details. So, with the exception of animation (technically an on-screen role), voice actors don't come with this sort of resume.

On-screen actors also need headshots or photos. In voiceover, photos aren't necessary either. The only time in which you would want to include photos of yourself, is when you sound exactly how you look. Not the way that you think you sound either. Only when your voice profile matches your headshots or photos should you brand/market your voice with your face. Why? Theater of the mind baby!

Voiceover is all about letting the audience's conscious imagination fill in the gaps. If I hear you as a brunette but you're blond, you just altered my creativity.

Anytime people can judge a book by its cover, they will. It's best to let perception be up to the ear of the beholder and not allow personal appearance to alter how someone envisions you based on your voice.

Make something from nothing: If you have a consistent client that is, let's say, a local Honda dealership. No one will care that you list John Doe Honda dealership under your voiceover credits.

Instead list the Honda brand under your credits, since that is what will ultimately stand out to an agent. By just listing Honda instead of the specific dealership, you are branding yourself better and omitting unnecessary information.

While on-screen actors must include the specific details of

their roles, voiceover credits are simpler. If you voiced for a Home Depot commercial, you don't need to list the exact character you played. Why? Because you performed voiceover for a Home Depot spot. That's all the prospective clients would want to know.

Agent Articles
A Word from Your Peers

We asked 100 of today's top voiceover talent what you can do to get an agent in a major market. It's a goal most talent hold high and it's important to know and understand exactly what agents in cities like NY, LA and Chicago are looking for. The results are below.

92% of the talent we interviewed said they have an outstanding demo and believe that demo played a huge role in the agent's decision to sign them.

Demos are mostly subjective but there are some simple, straight forward rules that allow a demo to exceed industry expectations.

First, research the standards for demos in the specific genres that interest you. Train with coaches that can explain these standards in detail. Never write your own copy. Use top quality national copy that is customized for your voice. Do not self-direct. Rely on the expert skills of a trained coach and lastly, do not self-produce. Hire a skilled producer who is known for their work on VO demos. 75% of the talent we interviewed said they have a great referral. It's important to have friends. Other VO talent are not only a wealth of hints and advice but they may be your ticket to a high powered agent.

Social websites like VoiceoverUniverse.com and live voiceover events and conferences will allow you to meet and mingle with talent that might become lasting friends and referrals. But choose wisely; a referral needs to be someone the agent works with and respects.

84% of the talent we interviewed said to have a great resume of coaches and instructors.

The right teachers are keys to your success. Each coach should have a clear area of expertise.

Research a coach's reputation within the industry and find out how well connected they are. Ask to interview former students as well.

One coach may not be all you need. Honestly, many talent find that training with a variety of coaches helps them to fast track their goal of landing a big agent.

Here's what else some of the voiceover talent we interviewed had to say about this question:

"...be persistent but not annoying and able to take criticism."
- Aly Steel

"... clear, concise branding."
- Mandy Kaplan

"Be brilliant! Pretty good won't get an agent. No one needs another voice. They have all the voices they will ever need. What they don't have is you. Your style, your heart, your sense of humor, your brain, your own individuality. Your brand. This is what will set you apart from everyone that the agent already represents. Your brand needs to be established within the first 4 seconds of your demo."
- Bob Bergen

"...prove that you can stick to it (the business) and not give up."
- Ian James Corlett

The Art of Voice Acting – on Agents

"One major advantage of having an agent to represent you is that you will gain access to auditions and clients that you might never have met if you were not represented. Your agent will also handle fee negotiations and collect payments.

It's their job to get you work, by sending you auditions and connecting you with producers who will hire you. Once on the audition, it becomes your job to perform to the best of your ability. Your agent only gets paid when you do. Your agent should also send your demo to casting directors, ad agencies, and production companies.

A talent agent is not in the business of nurturing you or grooming you to be a professional voice actor. A talent agent may not be interested in you unless you have a track record and an existing client list. You may have a great track record and an incredible demo, but you may get rejected simply because the agency already has other voice talent with the same or similar delivery style as yours. Being rejected for representation is not a personal attack on you or your performing abilities."

- James Alburger, The Art of Voice Acting 3rd Edition
Owner of The Voice Acting Academy in San Diego and Author of The Art of Voice Acting. His book is the most read and most widely regarded work on voice acting. For more than 35 years James has worked with voiceover artists as a director, performer and studio engineer in Los Angeles and San Diego.

Secret Agent Man
Sept. 2013 - Backstage.com

<u>How Agents Read Actor Submissions</u>

I hate Al Gore. The day that man invented the Internet, my life became a living hell. All the hard copy submissions were replaced by a deluge of emails that never seems to stop. Seriously, they come in every few minutes. There's no end.

I'm a curious cat, so I open every single one of those emails, just like I used to open all the hard copy submissions. A lot of agents ignore them, but that's not my nature. I have to know what's inside. Call it my tragic flaw.

So let's take a closer look at a recent submission from an actor named Brenda and my thought process as I read through it.

The email begins with a referral. On the surface, that's a good thing. One of the best ways to get an agent's attention is to have someone refer you. Doing this makes you stand out from the pack.

Unfortunately, this referral isn't going to work. Why? Because the person doing the referring is an acting teacher I've never met. The name doesn't even ring a bell, and I know a lot of teachers. Referrals from strangers are worthless.

Moving on, I see that Brenda's with a manager I don't like. Hell, no one likes this guy. He signs a ton of actors, places them with agents, and then completely ignores them. Instead of providing guidance, he lets people like me do all the heavy lifting. But rest assured, if there's an offer on the table, this manager suddenly becomes Johnny on the spot with opinions about the deal and how quickly he can receive his commission. I don't work with managers I don't like. At this point I already know I'm not interested in this actor, but hope springs eternal, so I decide to soldier on.

There are three headshots attached to the email. The first one is great. It shows an attractive young woman with dark hair and sky-blue eyes. The next picture isn't as impressive. The lighting's off, and her smile is as crooked as Lombard Street. I brace myself and click on the last one. Yikes! This picture is simply terrible. It's like the headshot of Dorian Gray. She should've quit while she was ahead.

Always go with your best picture, the one everyone loves. Burn the rest. (In Voiceover speak, this means go with your best demo/ audio sample - not necessary the most recent job.)

Well, Brenda has one last chance to redeem herself. Sure, the referral is nonsense and her manager's a joke, but she does have one decent picture and I still haven't looked at her résumé. This could all turn around with the click of a mouse. I decide to go for it. Click. The PDF opens, and I start to inspect the cluttered document.

She has 12 film credits, and I don't recognize any of them. That's not a good sign. They're all probably short films or glorified home movies. Either way, those "credits" mean nothing. (It's the same with Voiceover.)

Reading further, I see she's listed a series regular credit on a pilot that isn't real. It's probably some web thing no one has ever seen. Real pilots involve a studio and a network. The rest of her résumé is even less impressive. Here are a few random observations:

Brenda has eight theater credits, but I've never heard of the plays or the theaters where they were done. Her training section has one L.A. teacher I recognize. The rest are from out of town, and no, I'm not talking about New York or Chicago.

Under special skills I see "years of improv experience," but I don't see any improv under training. What's up with that? And that's all she wrote. This submission is a definite pass, but it's all good because another 20 came in while I was reading this one. Like I said, hope springs eternal…

How to Land Representation
Feb. 2012 - Backstage.com

The other night I was burning headshots for fun, and it occurred to me that I spend a lot of time in this column explaining all the reasons agents pass on actors.

Common sense dictates we don't pass on everyone because if that were true, agents wouldn't have any clients. And while that sounds peaceful, it's not practical. So this week, I'd like to explain why agents decide to take on actors, especially ones who don't have much experience.

First and foremost, it's about talent. This is still the number one way to end up on someone's client list. I've always felt too many actors focus on networking skills at the expense of craft. You definitely need both, but an actor without talent is like a Ferrari without an engine. Skill is what drives your career. All that other stuff's important, too, but it should always take a back seat to your actual acting ability.

(OK, I'm done with the car metaphors.) Next, we have type. Agents are basically sellers, and casting directors are buyers. It's our job to address that marketplace. No real agency focuses on any one specific type. That would be financial suicide. We sign all kinds of actors so we always have someone to submit for the roles.

Skill is something you work on in class. Type isn't. You are who you are. The key is to understand your type so you can exploit it. Are you the female lead or are you her best friend? Are you the guy who owns the bar, or are you the dude who drinks there? Knowing how you come across is important.

And don't worry about typecasting. You'll have plenty of chances to stretch when you're established. For now, it's important to understand how people see you and how that image fits into the marketplace. (This is the essence of the Voiceover business too, way to many voice actors fail to understand that having a specific sound is a good thing.)

Another reason agents say yes is that we spot the self-promoter gene in someone we're meeting. I love actors who are on their game, constantly pushing a new play while producing their web series between doing casting workshops. It tells me that if I sign this person, he's not going to sit around and let me do all the work.

On that same note, coming across as a professional is another excellent way to make an impression. I respect actors who hand me their pictures and résumés without excuses. If your headshot isn't up to par, then you're not ready to meet me. I don't want to hear, "Sorry, it's an old picture." That's just lame. Get your act together before.

You've probably heard a referral is the best way to get a meeting with an agent. That's absolutely true, but the referral only gets you in the room. It's not a guarantee you're going to get signed. But there have been times when I've been on the fence about someone and I ended up going forward anyway because of the person who referred them.

The final reason is a wild card. Every now and then, an actor will get signed because an agent likes them. Being able to connect on a personal level is an essential skill. Some actors are naturals at this. Others aren't. Either way, you shouldn't come across as wanting something from us. Instead, if you can present yourself as a real human being, it might just make all the difference in your career.

How to Make Friends and Influence Your Career
Jan. 2013 - Backstage.com

After a refreshing holiday break, I have mixed feelings about going back to work. Part of me is focused, already thinking ahead to the arrival of pilot season. But there's another part that's looking back, remembering the early days of my career.

I started as an assistant at one of the largest companies in the business. Back then, I could barely afford the suits I had to wear. My entire life consisted of answering phones, sending out auditions, and running errands for my boss.

Tired of working for slave wages, I realized the only way off that desk was to build a circle of contacts who could help me make the big move. Thanks to my job, I had access to the best casting directors in town, but I knew I couldn't just drop to my knees and beg. That kind of behavior gets you nowhere fast. So instead, I did my best to bond with them, always being professional, never asking for anything.

When the time was right, I shared my frustration. I asked for their advice on how to approach other agencies. They responded by making calls on my behalf. This led to several interviews and, eventually, the perfect offer.

Those casting directors helped me because they liked me. I never asked them to make those calls. They offered. And that's how I became an agent.

Now watch carefully, ladies and gentlemen, as I take this little history lesson and apply it to your life as an actor. There are no tricks up my sleeve, just common sense. A few months ago, I went to see a play at an established theater company in North Hollywood. When the show was over, my date went off to powder her nose while I waited in the lobby. That's when the cast started coming out. I spotted one actor who did an especially good job, so I went over to congratulate him.

At first, we had a pleasant conversation about the production, but when I mentioned what I did for a living, the guy turned desperate and started begging me to sign him. He didn't even know where I worked, but he kept coming at me, insisting that I give him a chance. Luckily, my date returned and pulled me away to safety.

But the story doesn't end there. Believe it or not, the actor actually followed us outside, creating an uncomfortable situation that bordered on creepy. I finally had to ask him to leave us alone.

This actor wasted an excellent opportunity. I just saw and liked his work. If he had played his cards right, he could've added me to his own circle of contacts. But no, he jumped the gun by asking me for representation. So in my eyes, he immediately turned into yet another actor who wants something from me.

What he should've done was follow the example I set as an assistant. All the actor had to do was thank me for attending the show. Then he could've followed up with an email that needs a response, something like this: "Thanks again for checking out our play. It's always a nice surprise when someone like you takes the time to see theater in this town. And by the way, I'm thinking about signing up for some casting workshops. Are there any companies you'd recommend?"

Since I was the one who approached him at the theater, the odds are I'm going to respond. And that's the start of a relationship, one the actor can exploit at a future time.

Learning how to approach and network with industry professionals should be an important part of your business plan. So don't be shy, but avoid being pushy. Find the sweet spot that allows you to build your own personal circle of contacts.

The Rules to Follow

Rule #1
Follow directions. Agents will tell you exactly how to submit your materials to them. Go to their websites FIRST. Pay close attention and find the posted talent submission information. Can't find what you need on their site? Call them BEFORE submitting. Failure to pay attention to details could cost you opportunities. Many agents will throw away submissions that fail to meet the agency's basic requirements. Why? Because you failed their first test; to see if you could follow basic instructions.

Rule#2
Look as good as you sound Be mindful of how you Brand yourself when submitting VO materials. Does your brand match your voice? Have you put the necessary work into developing a brand? If not, agent submissions may be premature. You are at your best when you can help an agent to see exactly what your top skills are and how the agent can best sell you.

Rule #3
Don't be desperate Nothing repels people, especially agents, more than the smell of desperation. Respect the fact that you have something valuable that you're bringing to the table. Be their partner, not a need- machine. Make them want to work with you or wonder why you don't need them. Make them think they need you.

Rule #4
Don't bug the f*** out of them Persistence is admirable, but there's definitely a thin line between persistence and irritating your way out of ever getting an agent to partner with you.

Rule #5

Know how to use a referral A referral needs to be someone an Agent works with and respects. This could be a fellow actor, existing client of theirs, a manager or creative director. Whoever it is, they must have an excellent reputation.

Rule #6

Don't suck Develop your skills as a voice actor by practicing, working with a coach, and attending classes/workshops. Don't just be good - be a humble, well-educated student of your craft.

Don't be the talent that...

(A) Pesters the sh*t out of an agent about: - Payment on a job - The status of an audition - the few dozen questions you have prior to answering an audition

Doing so only irritates them and frankly hurts their feelings. This is the business they are in. An agent has no reason to: withhold money, withhold whether or not you booked, or withhold details that would help you land a gig.

(B) Responds to EVERY audition sent to you. Why not?

You don't want to: - Have a poor or low booking ratio in relation to the number of auditions you answer. - Make your agent think that you're not carefully selecting gigs.

(C) Responds to every gig that you are NOT interested in.

This will eventually cause your agent to stop sending you auditions and or drop you from their roster. Plus it wastes unnecessary amounts of time.

How to Find Agents

They really aren't hard to find. The voiceover industry has a good number of resources you can acquire to help you.

1. VoiceBank.net - is an online casting directory that clients use to find voices. Agents who are part of VoiceBank pay an annual fee to have their talent roster listed. You can learn a good deal about the agents on VoiceBank simply by viewing their roster and profile page.

2. Call Sheet by Backstage (formerly the Ross Report) is a leading acting resource both in print and online form. It's a must-have tool for on-camera and theater actors and it lists close to 800 agents nationwide.

You can use the directory to research an agent, their specialty, what they rep for and how they like to receive submissions. This is a labor intensive process but a worthwhile one for the extremely budget conscious.

3. Other voiceover actors are one of your best resources. Start paying attention to who reps who. And as you meet new voiceover actors find out who their agents are (mostly by snooping on their websites). You'll see some clear patterns emerge as to what type of talent a particular agent likes and which agents are the most active in their signing efforts.

Notes: *Use the space below to write notes, questions or reminders related to agents*

_____
_____
_____
_____

Lightning Source UK Ltd.
Milton Keynes UK
UKHW02f1447170718
325828UK00007B/670/P